Common Sense Advice

Simple Stories for Success
In Business and Organizations

Helene F Uhlfelder PhD

Helene F Uhlfelder PhD

All rights reserved.

No part of this book may be reproduced or transmitted in any form or by any means, electronic or mechanical, including photocopying, recording, or by any information storage and retrieval system, without permission in writing from the author or publisher: Purple Zebra Productionz, LLC.

Helene F Uhlfelder PhD
(404) 307-8926
helenefuhlfelder@gmail.com
www.helenefuhlfelder.com
1449 Harmott Ave.
Norfolk, VA 23509

Articles were previously published in *Inside Business and are used with their permission.*

ISBN: 978-1537631103

Introduction For New Version

The first version of this book, *Simple Stories for Success*, was published in 2007. Although almost a decade has passed, the stories and lessons in this book still hold true. I find myself using the same tools with and giving similar advice to current clients.

It is disheartening to know that concepts like "total quality" and "process improvement" are no longer part of the business environment. It's not just the language missing, but the day-to-day use of management principles that had a proven track record for improving business performance Such as balanced scorecards, performance feedback, and team management.

My goals for re-publishing this book are to remind people about these concepts and practices; to refresh people' memories; and educate new managers and leaders. Although much has changed in the business world, "old" practices can be modified to fix the current work world.

Introduction

The format of this book was driven by a comment made to me by a client. The CEO told me: "Never send me anything longer than two pages because I will not read it." The stories in this book are not all two pages, but they are short enough to read quickly.

These articles were originally published in *Inside Business,* The Hampton Roads business journal owned by The Virginian-Pilot in Norfolk, VA, and are published here with their permission.

My goals with these columns were and continues to be to provide entertaining stories that illustrate good examples of what it takes to be successful as a business and bad examples of what companies do that hamper success. These stories apply to all types of organizations. Some of the columns tell stories about non-profits; others describe for-profit businesses' examples. The stories are about dance groups, plumbers, government entities, Fortune 500 companies, and many other types of organizations.

The columns are sometimes humorous, sometimes sad, but always educational and practical. Although based on sound theories from psychology, business, management, and science, the stories are real and provide helpful suggestions for how you can improve your business or organization.

I am sharing my *Common Sense Advice* with you to share with your organization. They make great starting points for conversation and dialogue about, "How can we be more successful as an organization?"

Enjoy!

Table Of Contents

New Computers Won't Help If You Don't Plan	9
Simple Solutions Are Often Painless But Pointless	12
For Every Action There's A Reaction	15
When Culture Blocks Change, It's Time To Re-evaluate	17
Getting It Right The First Time	20
Strategic Planning – Worth The Effort Or Not?	23
Borderless Teams Need New Rules	26
How To Get The Most From Your Teams	29
Leaders Have Hard Time Functioning As A Team	31
A Silo Mentality Can Hurt Most Organizations	34
Design An Organization Around The Customers	37
Good Management Alters The Need To Restructure	40
There's An Art To Restructuring	43
Get Rid Of The Walls And Floors	45
Recognize Work Boundaries, But Keep Them Fluid	47
Knowing The Rules Of Partnering Can Pay Off	50
Withholding Information Costs Ultimate Price	53
Measurement Can Be A Four-letter Word	55

Here's A Script That Wins Applause	58
The Dance Became A Business Lesson	60
Does Your Organization Give And Take Feedback?	63
A Lesson In How To Make A Great Leader	66
Resolve Conflict By Process Improvement	68
Saying Thank You Improves Performance	70
When Public Conflict Swamps Your Boat	73
I've Never Seen So Many Men Shopping	75
Reversing A Nosedive	77
Remove The Emotion When Change Is Afoot	80
Innovative Companies Just Don't Happen, They're Created	83
Why I Bought Another Handbag	86
What A Difference A Human Being Makes	88
Sensitivity Training Needs To Be Revisited	91
Consultants Should Have Expertise Warning Labels	94
Love Your Work And Love Your Team	96
Even If All Is Well, It Can Get Better	98
Transformation Requires A Change Champion	101
About Whole Systems	104
Creating Alignment Of The Whole System	105

Team Systems: Why Teams?	108
Managing Change for Business Transformation	111
About The Author	113

Helene F Uhlfelder PhD

New Computers Won't Help If You Don't Plan

Did you know that companies abandon forty-two percent of all information-technology projects before completion and that seventy-five percent of companies experience less productivity for as long as a year after implementing enterprise-based software?

Millions of dollars are lost on redundant systems and lower productivity. Organizations lose worker goodwill and trust. Shareholder value is reduced. Time and resources are wasted. Each time a new information technology or information system effort fails, skepticism and resistance increase, making it harder to engage people the next time.

Why do such technological efforts fail? All failures, no matter what the company or industry, result from one of these reasons: The projects often have no clear connection to the organization's strategy. Companies often lack a compelling, clearly articulated reason for changes. If you are asking people to disrupt their normal work patterns, do their work differently, and change their normal behavior, there better be good reasons to do so. Not only do people need to know the reasons for changes, they need to know how the changes will help the organization, the customers, or most important, themselves.

The second common cause of failure is a lack of active, visible leadership. Organizations tend to begin technology projects believing that only the information department needs to lead the effort. The larger and more complex the undertaking, the more the business leaders and company executives need to champion the change.

Thirdly, managers tend to forget communicating with and involving all stakeholders and users until the installation is nearly finished. Failures to communicate will stop a new computer system in its tracks.

Fourth, piecemeal approaches to information-technology initiatives and failure to redesign work patterns doom such a project even before you turn on the first monitor. The best computer systems are powerless to fix problems with work and collaborations that make no sense. Often this conflict between the organization's culture and its outdated practices with the capability of the new system produces real problems.

Last, many organizations provide training too early, too late, or not at all. If you have tried to learn how to use new software, you have experienced how this affects your productivity. In companies that make this mistake, you find people using old tools, such as their own Excel spreadsheets rather than the PeopleSoft system it just bought, to do their work.

All is not hopeless: Your outfit can be in the good 25 percent. Managers must use good common sense. Unfortunately, most organizations believe technology fixes everything, and they do not have the discipline to complete basic risk-reduction activities. The successful companies answer two basic questions: "How do we manage the implementation so we are on time and budget?" and "What work processes, managerial practices, or human resource processes do we need to modify to get the most from our investment?" To answer the first question, successful companies address:

- Leadership: Leaders actively demonstrate their understanding of and commitment to the system and its impact on the business.

- Communication: All managers and workers have the opportunity to be involved in the project early on.

- Measurement: There is a clear connection between performance measures, such as customer-response time or customer service, and the project. In addition, measures are in place to monitor adherence to budget and time goals.

- o Motivation: Consideration is given to additional ways to reward people for acceptance and use of new systems. Management punishes stubborn people who fail to adapt to the new system.

- o Motivation: Consideration is given to additional ways to reward people for acceptance and use of new systems. Management punishes stubborn people who fail to adapt to the new system.

- o Skills and capabilities: Assess what skills and capabilities people will need to work with the new system and provide timely, targeted education, training and coaching.

Successful organizations also redesign processes and practices to fit business strategies and new systems. This demonstrates that managers understand that technology enables improved performance, but that it is not an end unto itself.

Each company is different so the actions taken depend on its past history and resources. A simple path of assess, plan, execute, monitor and modify can be developed and followed.

Helene F Uhlfelder PhD

Simple Solutions Are Often Painless But Pointless

Over the past few months, I met with leaders from several organizations in diverse industries about issues each organization faces in its respective market space. The leaders sought recommendations for how to approach their issues and how to achieve some specific business result through a planned improvement effort.

As I listened to the leaders and asked questions, it struck me that in each case, the client wanted an answer, a simple solution to a complex problem. One, for example, wanted to increase and sustain market share in an industry where the company was not the market leader. This company, believing it knew the answer, wanted to redesign its sales and marketing process. "I know if we had a repeatable selling and marketing process and we had a strong relationship with our customers, we would be able to achieve our market-share goals," the project manager insisted.

When questioned about other factors that influence market share, he insisted that those other factors did not matter, just the sales and marketing process and telling salespeople they had to be relationship managers in the future. FYI: This company had a long history of starting improvement projects, beginning implementation, then abruptly ending one project and starting another when results did not occur immediately.

With a different client, the issue was how to persuade people to use measurement to manage the business. In this case, the VP believed that providing training on scorecards and measures was the answer to the problem. This particular organization had a history of implementing change at the front-line level but was unable to induce senior managers to change their behaviors and attitudes. The project manager wanted a solution that worked with general employees but did not require any change from managers and leaders.

In these two cases and in several more, it struck me that organizations still believe in the Lone Ranger and the silver bullet: Give us the answer in a single solution, all will be fixed, and you can ride out of town. From experience, I knew that neither organization would be successful if each continued to view its issues through a single lens. Both organizations' issues were complex, had multiple causes, and required systemic, integrated solutions. Instead of a simple solution, what should each organization do?

In the case of the market-share problem, the company decided to take a more holistic approach. It started by gathering information about internal and external factors that influenced business and ultimately market share. After confirming that the root causes for the problems were not just in the sales and marketing process, the company developed a comprehensive solution that focused on improved processes, changes to performance feedback and rewards systems, and an implementation plan that focused on short-term and long-term behavior change.

However, this did not happen without pain and confusion. "Why can't we just pick the two or three key problems and fix those?" lamented one project team member. Another complained, "I hate this process work. Why do we have to define a process? We have gotten along for years without a consistent one."

The second company has a more senior issue to confront. Without management's and leadership's active commitment to and involvement in any improvement effort, the rest of the organization can improve only so much. Yes, you can have some incremental improvement, but lasting and continuous improvement depends on what leaders bring -- clear direction, commitment of resources such as time, money and people, and visible behavior that shows the rest of the organization their personal investment in the process and the results.

In this case, a simple solution would be to provide training and support to the front-line employees and avoid conflict or confrontation with the leaders. My bet is that the results from the simple solution would be disappointing and employees continually would point out how their managers were not involved or supportive. Simple solutions can work short-term, but ultimately, the tough, more complex issues will need to be addressed for long-term success.

For Every Action There's A Reaction

Two recent incidents reminded me that organizations, in their efforts to correct one problem, sometimes implement solutions that create new and equally problematic consequences. One example: A government organization with a history of favoritism and a lack of open competition for all vendors developed a new process for soliciting bids and awarding contracts. Three principles of their approach were: speed through the use of automation and quantitative analyses; lower costs through fostering high levels of competition between vendors and setting requirements for vendors to carry all travel expenses; and sparse RFP documents based on the notion that the vendors should supply their solutions as a way to prove their competence and previous experience.

The new process guaranteed fast cycle time, did not depend on interaction between the client and the vendor prior to selection (to reduce favoritism and cronyism), and claimed that value, not low costs, was the deciding factor.

The department responsible for developing and managing the procurement process was measured on cost savings and the number of different vendors that were utilized in a calendar year. Clients and vendors were asked to rate satisfaction with the process but these ratings were not considered as important as costs and competition. Several years after implementing the new process, many people were complaining. Clients were frustrated with their chosen vendors once the vendor started working, as there were large gaps between expectations and delivery due to lack of specificity in the RFPs.

Problems with "chemistry" between the client and the vendor caused delays, rework and frustration as the human factor was not quantifiable, and people had not met before the contract was signed. Small businesses were driven out of the process due to the fact they could not cover all employee expenses. Various internal groups felt stifled by a lack of flexibility in how they wrote their RFPs and whether they got to keep their incumbent contractor or not due to the new rules. Neither internal clients nor vendors were happy with the process, but the department responsible for the process was rewarded because they could show cost reductions and high levels of competition.

The second example occurred with a publicly held company. To reduce overall costs, the company decided to move its customer service function offshore because salaries in India and China were much lower than the wages and benefits paid to local employees. In addition, money traditionally spent on employee development was cut from the budget as training and development were viewed as nice-to-do but not essential to the company's current profit goals. With a very tight job market, the company did not fear employee turnover.

As a result of these decisions, employees who were left after all the changes were demoralized. Although people did not quit, their commitment to the company and their levels of discretionary effort decreased. The unemployed people who used to spend money on company products in their local communities, no longer had the funds to do this, which negatively influenced the local economy.

Remember the saying that for every action there is a reaction. To avoid the pendulum effect, it is imperative to think through intended and unintended consequences of any solution or decision. Think about how organizations are part of other interdependent systems such as communities and business networks and how it is impossible to drastically change one part of the whole without affecting all other parts of the whole.

Before you implement any solution, ask yourself: If this new process is successful, what consequences or outcomes – both positive and negative – might occur? Always leave room for open feedback and allow flexibility to modify the solution if negative consequences are noted. And finally, reward, do not punish, the people who speak up early and provide data to warn of possible undesirable outcomes.

When Culture Blocks Change, It's Time To Re-evaluate

Most management books and experts talk about how important culture is for creating and sustaining high-performance organizations. The reverse trend is also notable: organizations with cultures that limit innovation and growth. It seems to me that the present economic and business conditions are bringing out the negative side of this equation more than the positive.

Here are a couple of examples. A large division of a well-known business is having trouble gaining and sustaining market share. After years of attempting to correct this trend on their own, the president and his leaders contracted with outside consultants to help them uncover the root causes of the problem and develop fresh solutions to try and turn this trend around.

Each time a new approach or new idea was surfaced by the outsiders, "cultural excuses" were given.

- "Most of our people have been here 35 years or more. Their parents and grandparents worked here. There is no way you can understand us and our business until you see things the way we do."

- We have great process experts. We don't need anyone looking at our processes because we know we have the best and brightest."

- "No one disagrees with the president. Everyone has several pre-meetings with him to get him on your side, and then you can't count on his not changing his mind in the middle of the meeting."

- "If you don't do things the way we think they should be done, we won't allow you to continue working with us."

These and dozens more examples keep this organization from seeing new ways to work that might solve its market-share problem. This organization is doomed to repeat its mistakes until it can honestly hear outside viewpoints and understand that part of the root cause for its problem is the inability to appreciate viewpoints and ideas "not invented here."

Another example is of a very successful service organization that is trying to grow in size, both with number of clients and consultants. The people in this organization rigidly adhere to cultural guidelines such as:

- "Most important is that you are nice."

- "Never confront."

- "Everyone we hire must be just like us; we cannot tolerate people who behave differently than the founders."

- "Our clients come to us because of our culture, and we must mold everyone to our image."

Although this organization has done a good job of attracting new clients and new consultants, turnover in both areas is high. The executives are so focused on maintaining the status quo, they are driving away people with new ideas and clients whose needs may have changed in the past two years.

Both of these organizations have many fine qualities and are made up of dedicated people who want to be successful. The challenge both have is related to culture. How rigidly should an organization stick to its culture? When does an organization's culture need to be re-examined to ascertain a match with the current environment? Is it really the formal culture that is the problem? Or is the real problem the behaviors that have been in place so long that no one has questioned if they really reflect the intent of the cultural parameters?

What can organizations do to make sure the culture does not become an inhibitor for growth and change?

First, a strong commitment to hearing the truth must be in place. Second, insiders and outsiders must be allowed to point out situations where the organization's past practices may be a narrow interpretation of the culture and the reason for lack of sustainable growth and change. Third, an organization must be willing to keep the best parts of the culture and equally willing to adapt the culture. Lastly, it must be willing to provide resources to train and coach people on new behaviors.

Helene F Uhlfelder PhD

Getting It Right The First Time

While working with a client to complete the organization's balanced scorecard, I had an "ah-ha" moment. The leadership team members decided that one of their critical measures had to be "Right First Time," and this measure would be one that combined all manufacturing's percentage of how many of their products were produced without errors.

It was obvious the only way this company could meet its clients' supply demands and reduce costs was to do things right the first time.

As I observed their decision-making processes, their implementation of a variety of initiatives, and the leadership team's approach to and processes for managing the business, it was obvious that "Right First Time" only applied to manufacturing, not any of the other processes, especially theirs. For example, this team completed two days of leadership team formation where the team learned and practiced the skills needed to function in a team environment.

They were actively facilitated through processes to define the team's mission, to create shared roles and responsibilities, to develop a site balanced scorecard, and to set goals and provide consequences for desired and undesired behaviors. At the end of the session, 100 percent of the leaders found the two days extremely valuable. The members acknowledged that they could not have completed as much as they did without the two days of training and facilitation.

One of the decisions the leadership team made was to implement the use of a balanced scorecard throughout the organization. When it was time to do this, they basically said, "Just go meet with the leader, have him or her decide the measures, and tell them they need to utilize the scorecard to manage their portion of the business."

One of the decisions the leadership team made was to implement the use of a balanced scorecard throughout the organization. When it was time to do this, they basically said, "Just go meet with the leader, have him or her decide the measures, and tell them they need to utilize the scorecard to manage their portion of the business."

There was not mention of completing team formation sessions for any of the next levels of teams.

I challenged them on why they would not require team formation sessions for the next level of teams. "We don't have the time nor do we want to pay for this," was the reply they gave me. It was not until they were told that the teams would not know what to do and that a great deal of time, energy and good-will would be lost, that they reluctantly agreed to "try and get the sessions into their schedule." I explained that if the process was implemented correctly, people would utilize the scorecard appropriately and that the odds for improvement were highly increased. I asked, "Why would you not do this right the first time? Why would you do something poorly and create rework? Do you not have a measure 'right first time' for the manufacturing operation? Does this measure not apply to you?"

They were stunned. They had never considered the fact that producing error-free processes applied to them. Although reluctant to say that every team needed help to implement the next steps, they agreed to have some type of team development sessions for the next level of leadership team.

When told it would take external help and internal resources to do this right, they balked again. Their stance was, "We are extremely intelligent people. Why do we need to spend money on external resources? And why can't it be done in two hours?"

I had to explain that if they did not do the implementation correctly, they would waste time, waste money and reinforce the cultural practice of "never finish anything." I also explained how much more difficult it is to unlearn wrong behaviors and learn new behaviors than it is to learn and do something right the first time.

Helene F Uhlfelder PhD

If as you read this you recognize your company, try the following: Ask yourself, "What is the long-term cost of doing this right the first time? What is the long-term cost of not doing it right?" The answers to these questions should be obvious, and you will end up making the right choice.

Strategic Planning – Worth The Effort Or Not?

It must be that time of year when organizations decide to create, revisit or update their strategic plans. The reason I suspect this is because I have had multiple requests from for-profit and nonprofit organizations to talk about strategic planning. Someone on the board of a local nonprofit made a comment that I believe reflects how many people feel about the strategic planning process.

She said, "I am not sure doing strategic planning is worth the time and money because in all my years on boards and having my own business, I have never seen a strategic plan turned into implementation, action and results." Sadly, I had to agree with her about many organizations' lack of follow-through on the specific operational actions needed to make a strategic plan a living document.

As a strong proponent of strategic planning as a necessary step in creating and sustaining successful and competitive organizations, I educate my clients on how to make the process and the plan useful. The following ideas are ones you and your organization should consider when developing your strategic plan:

1. Take a whole-system perspective beginning with external influences and trends. To create a plan that is dynamic and reflects all the influences outside of the organization's boundaries, you must consider what is happening in the larger world, the economy, technology trends, competitors' behaviors, customer and non-customer trends and desires, and local business conditions. By understanding the external forces, you are More likely to create a strategic plan that is designed for flexibility and adaption as conditions change. In addition, make sure the process includes steps to examine all aspects of the organization metrics, work processes, use

of technology, organization structure, roles and responsibilities, capabilities development, and consequences practices (rewards, recognition, feedback, etc.) Changes in one part of the organization will have impacts on all other parts of the organization, and it's better to plan for these impacts rather than leaving them to chance.

2. Involve the people who will need to implement the plan in the planning process. It is well known that the more that people believe they had input to a plan, the more likely it is that they will feel a sense of ownership and a commitment to implement the ideas. This does not mean everyone must be involved, but efforts should be made to get as many stakeholders, associates, managers and external resources as possible. Some organizations ask individual departments or teams to create their plans first, then the leaders use that input to develop the organization's strategic plan.

3. Write the plan with implementation in mind. The strategic plan is really just a starting point from which operational tactics and actions are developed. The best plans I have seen have been written so that everyone can understand what is important, what critical actions need to be taken in the coming three, six, nine and 12 months. The plan also clearly states how progress will be measured and which key organizational indices are expected to change. Another critical practice is to not write strategic and tactical plans unless resources are available to actually implement the plans. I have read many plans that have page after page of specific actions the organization intends to implement, but no plan for how to resource each action. It is far better to plan fewer actions and provide resources for implementation than to have long lists of actions that will never be fully resourced.

4. Refer to and use the plan in communications. For the plan to be seen as a living document, you must regularly use the plan. Refer to it in communications; talk about how various actions taken relate to the plan and its objectives and goals. Modify or institute organizational scorecards that can be used to track, monitor and reinforce progress toward particular goals. Use the plan to provide positive and corrective feedback to people, e.g., "Your helping with that project really moved the ball forward on reaching our goal as described in this year's plan."

Strategic planning does not have to be a boring three-day session from which a document is developed and placed on a shelf until next year. Try some of these ideas and see if your organization's plan can be a useful tool for improving organizational performance.

Helene F Uhlfelder PhD

Borderless Teams Need New Rules

Have you been on an airplane lately and talked to the people sitting next to you? If you have, you probably discovered the fact that very few businesspeople are co-located with the rest of their organization -- even now when many businesses are using non-essential business travel as a way to lower costs.

Have you been on a project team lately? Most people have been, as more organizations form teams across functional boundaries to complete assignments and accomplish day-to-day work. What do all these situations have in common? They all represent virtual organizations. Virtual organizations are borderless. They represent new configurations not based on static space or simultaneous time. People can work from different locations, at different times, and for different functions, businesses or companies.

But how do you manage this new type of organization? What are the major challenges and how do you address them?

Old management practices, outdated technologies and traditional processes will not work in the virtual organization. Processes and systems must be agile and flexible and provide continuity and shared purpose. Work processes, human resource practices and information technology should be designed to support people and teams working time zones and cultures apart, yet needing to be in "close" contact. The ability to discuss problems, develop solutions and come to consensus decisions under these conditions does not come without planning, commitment and a willingness to try new behaviors.

But of all the challenges facing virtual organizations, the most critical one is: How do you build trust among people who never see each other face-to-face? Or who speak a different language?

How do you create a high-performance team when time and space are working against you?

One given is that you must use technology effectively. This includes everything from teleconferencing and webcasts to the databases and information systems available to all members of the team and key stakeholders. Additionally, job definitions should include clear expectations and rewards for working in virtual situations. A third given is that the old way people got to know each other and feel comfortable (e.g., spending face-to-face time during the day, having lunch together, attending meetings each week) is not available anymore. By not having these known, proven ways of building trust, many companies falter when trying to use virtual means for getting work done.

Here are some additional actions your organization can take to improve how well virtual teams or groups perform:

- Set up multiple ways for people to communicate (e-mail, chat rooms, bulletin boards and knowledge management systems as well as phone calls) and reinforce people utilizing all of them.

- Set clear guidelines for all members of the team relating to issues such as team members talking among themselves, not just on full-team calls, and the team leader contacting each member of the team on a regular basis.

- Set clear guidelines and goals for the "project" or the work: Use a set of measures that reflect progress and final success. Make sure the team members get reinforcement for steps along the way as well as final results.

- All calls, webcasts, etc. should have an agenda that goes out in advance. The agenda should include some short team-building activity so members get to know each other. Have different members of the team take responsibility for parts of the agenda and work.

- Be respectful of people's time zone by varying the times when calls take place. Record calls, telecasts, etc. for future use. That way people can catch up on their own time.

- If at all possible, bring the team together once, at the beginning of the project or once a year if it is an ongoing effort.

It is not impossible to have a successful virtual team or organization. Many organizations have become quite successful being virtual (universities and colleges) by providing their customers with products and services to meet the customers' schedule. It just takes a little extra effort and planning.

How To Get The Most From Your Teams

Teams, whether they are virtual, project or natural work teams, have been shown as a very effective way for companies to fully engage their workforce. Not every team is successful, but there are some actions and behaviors we know can increase the likelihood of teams being so. Read this list and assess whether your teams are doing these things or not. If the teams are not consistently completing these actions, refocus and coach them.

Teams need to be part of an articulated business strategy that has financial or other success targets. The organization's senior leadership needs to be able to articulate and measure essential business indications it wants the teams to improve. Otherwise, teams are wandering, making up projects on which to work and hoping to see success. The difference between the companies who link teams to real business problems and those that don't is simply stated: It is success.

Each team needs to know its purpose and how it fits into the rest of the organization. What are the team's special roles and responsibilities? All teams must know their roles and responsibilities and how they align with the other teams' in the organization. Leadership teams should take time and review all teams' purpose statements to check for redundancies, gaps and alignment. Companies that check and align team purposes, roles and responsibilities waste less time on meaningless activities and redundant work.

Every team needs to meet regularly to review its scorecard and performance against its measures as well as to complete any team assignments. The focus of meetings should be on performance review and problem solving, not just on sharing information.

Team members should be able to read and interpret measurement graphs and explain how their work influences each measure. Companies that focus their meeting time hear fewer complaints about wasted time in meetings.

Team members need interpersonal, work-related and business skills to function well. This means team members need training, coaching and feedback about how they perform on the skills to do their jobs and work as team members. The companies that provide adequate and ongoing training achieve better results than those that do not plan for this.

Team members and leaders must be held accountable for achieving results. When teams do well, they need positive reinforcement. When the team struggles, it needs corrective feedback and training. When teams refuse to cooperate, they need corrective feedback. Occasionally, they need discipline. This common failure is seen more often in companies that are not achieving the results they want.

Leadership teams must lead by example and action. Teams at the top should not be exempt from practicing teamwork and using the team as a way to manage and lead the organization. The most successful organizations have true teamwork at the top.

Be willing to assess and change systems to help the teams.

Antiquated or broken people systems – for example, compensation, information sharing and decision making – or work systems – for example, process steps, equipment and technical procedures – can prevent teams from achieving results. Analyze and correct these systems in an integrated way that aligns with the organization's business strategy and goals. Effective and efficient teams and teamwork are critical in today's highly competitive environment. Too many organizations fail to follow these suggestions. This causes workers and managers to be skeptical of the benefits of teams. Make sure your organization is not one of these.

Common Sense Advice

Leaders Have Hard Time Functioning As A Team

I gave a speech at a meeting of the local ASTD (American Society of Training and Development) several weeks ago. The topic was "Teams: A Dead Concept or the Future of Organizations?"

At the beginning of the speech, I asked the attendees to raise their hands if their organizations have used some type of team in the last few years. Almost 100 percent of the people raised their hands. I told them to keep their hands up if their organization had seen results from the teams they had put in place. About 50 percent put their hands down.

The next question was, "Does your organization have some type of scorecard with measures that show team performance?" About twenty percent kept their hands raised. The last question was, "How many of your organizations' leadership groups act like teams and demonstrate teamwork as a leadership team?" Three people had their hands raised, and one of them joked that his boss was sitting next to him, so he had to raise his hand.

Ironically, the informal research I did at that speech appears to mirror the same trends I see in business and industry in general. Even after 20-some years of rhetoric about and application of teams as a viable organizational practice, not much has changed. Just like the fact that most organizations have not completely implemented all aspects of new IT/IS systems to gain full competitive advantage, organizations haven not implemented all aspects of team systems to gain full benefits.

The speech's bottom line was that teams are not only still an appropriate model for how organizations can work more effectively and efficiently, present conditions make the concept of teams even more relevant. In today's world, where companies form partnerships and alliances outside of the core company and where they outsource portions of their functions, creating teamwork with diverse companies and other organizations must be part of the strategy for successful relationships.

As the participants at the speech demonstrated, there are still two major areas that can be mined for positive results: team scorecards and leadership teams demonstrating team behavior. Teams must have a visible balanced set of metrics to help them focus on how is the team's performance impacting critical organizational success indicators such as customer satisfaction, costs containment, process cycle time, product quality, employee development, innovation and revenue production. Every team and every member of the team should be able to tell you how the team's and the person's behavior impacts those critical indices.

Probably tied for importance to measures is the necessity of leadership groups to commit to demonstrating teamwork and to practice it in how they develop and implement strategies, make decisions, provide direction, monitor results and provide motivation. This is not the same as adding "teamwork" to the organization's vision and mission poster.

This involves first, stating clearly what teamwork means. How does teamwork show up in observable behavior? How will the leaders behave differently when they communicate with employees, shareholders and customers? How will teamwork be measured at the leadership level and the team level? Will recognition and reward systems be redesigned to reinforce team and individual behavior?

The reason leadership teams are often the hardest groups to change to team-based behavior is that in most organizations, one becomes a leader by demonstrating excellence in individual behaviors. Most leadership teams are comprised of individuals who over the years have shown what he or she can do for each person's department or group. Helping these people see the benefits for everyone by including the team focus is one good tactic for helping leadership teams make the transition from individual contributor to team contributor.

Provide examples of successful organizations. Provide education and coaching focused on helping the leaders win and achieve goals that are important to the leader based on teamwork. This is not an impossible task. I have been fortunate to watch organizations and their leaders embrace a team-based culture, go through the pain of changing, and finally see bottom-line results for the organization, its employees and themselves. It's worth the effort.

Helene F Uhlfelder PhD

A Silo Mentality Can Hurt Most Organizations

Here is a quick diagnostic to determine if siloed thinking is hurting your organization's performance and promoting internal competition vs. collaboration.

Is the Finance department responsible for managing the numbers for your organization? Is the IT department responsible for technology, information systems, and how information is used to make decisions? Is the Human Resources department responsible for anything that contains the words "human" or "organization?" Is Sales solely responsible for business development and Marketing for marketing?

For most organizations the answer to these questions is, "Yes, but isn't that their responsibility?" Unfortunately, once one department takes on one of these areas as their responsibility, the rest of the organization can deflect any responsibility for these critical functions. I experienced a very good example of this a few weeks ago while meeting with the CFO of a Fortune 500 company. We were discussing how to improve bottom-line performance, and I suggested several options including team process improvement, full utilization of scorecards throughout the organization, and possible restructuring of some departments. The CFO's first response was, "We have some people in HR that deal with these people issues. They can train people on how to do these activities. Actually, we have done some training on business process redesign, but we did not see any real results."

As I asked questions about why the leaders want to improve performance, I probed for what critical business indices the organization hoped to improve. Most of the CFO's answers related to areas such as cost reduction, customer satisfaction, and profit. I used this opportunity to point out that these measures pertained to more than just human resources issues and they really related to operations. I then asked, "If these are operational issues, who should be responsible for improving the organization's performance in these critical areas?"

Slowly, it dawned on the CFO that by throwing the responsibility over the wall from operations to HR, operations and other departments could blame HR if performance did not improve.

Here's another example of how that way of thinking can hurt the customer.

Several years ago I worked with a manufacturing company that was having a very difficult time meeting its customers' quality requirements. As customer complaints increased, more and more pressure was placed on the sales organization to handle the problems directly with customers and to beat up manufacturing for not doing a good job. The walls between sales and manufacturing grew higher and higher, and quality problems increased to the point that major customers were threatening to buy elsewhere.

In this company, the responsibility for customer satisfaction was sales' responsibility, and manufacturing personnel rarely saw the customers or heard about specific complaints. It took several months and hours of discussion among the leadership team and the various functional areas to realize that until sales and manufacturing broke down some of the historic walls and barriers, the problems would never be fixed. Specific tactics such as shared measures, regular meetings and feedback between organizations, and total organization incentives were implemented to improve the product quality and increase customer satisfaction.

There are some basic steps your organization can take to first assess how siloed your organization is and decide what you can do to begin to break down the walls and increase internal cooperation and collaboration. First, the senior leadership team should take time to examine how the organization's measures, structure, and recognition and reward systems are reinforcing siloed behavior. Second, serious consideration should be given to redesigning departments' and teams' roles and responsibilities to include more shared responsibilities. Third, institute some form of regular internal and external customer feedback that is openly shared with all affected people and departments. And finally, hold people and groups accountable for providing holistic solutions that don't just fix problems in one functional area and cause problems for others.

Design An Organization Around The Customers

My health insurance company recently switched from its previous home-delivery prescription provider to a new one owned and managed by its own parent company. Usually when this type of change occurs, the motivation is to save money, not to provide better service to the customer. While attempting to get a prescription refill problem fixed, I was reminded that many organizations continue to ignore basic good organization design principles when they create new businesses. Two of these principles are:

- Design work processes to eliminate redundancies and rework.

- Design the organization's structure around the whole process and with the customer in mind.

My recent experience provides a classic example of how having the right processes and technology in place and designing the structure (and roles and responsibilities) correctly could have saved the company time and money and kept the customer satisfied.

I had ordered a refill on some allergy medicine that comes in small bottles. With all previous orders, the medicine was wrapped in bubble wrap and shipped in a cardboard small box. This time, the bottles were sent in a flimsy envelope, and during shipment, the bottles were broken resulting in a wet package and no useable medicine.

When trying to get a replacement order sent to me, I discovered that – after four phone calls and 24 hours – exactly how the problem happened and how poorly designed the organization is to handle any type of customer complaint. The first person who answered my call placed me on hold and never returned. The second person could not find my member number, phone number or Rx number in his computer system. (I found out the reason for this the next day.) The third call handler found my information but was not allowed to resolve the problem, and had to transfer me to another department (the reshipping department) that was in another building. Unfortunately, the reshipping department was experiencing an unusual amount of calls, so an e-mail was going to have to be sent to them asking them to please contact me. I was reassured that someone would call me that evening. The person on the phone said that she did not have access to the reshipping information, that she could not authorize a reshipment and that someone else would have to tell me what happens next.

    The next day, after no follow-up call, I called the customer service number again. I talked to a fourth person who had trouble finding me in the system and said, "We got new software with new screen options and I can't find information anymore." When this person still could not answer my questions, I asked to speak to a supervisor. I was told that the supervisors were in another building and that I should wait while the call was transferred.

    You probably know the rest of the story: I waited 15 minutes for the supervisor and was told that reshipments took longer than regular refills. I was told I should go back to my doctor for a sample of the prescription because it would be five to ten days before I would receive my medicine. The supervisor ended the call with no apology but with "this is how our system works. You should have ordered your medicine earlier." Several common-sense business practices would have alleviated these problems: Redesigning the process from ordering through shipping as a whole end-to-end process to eliminate redundancies (not piecemeal like the organization is structured); automating the process and making sure all relevant customer information is captured in one place with easy-to-use screens; designing the structure so that people who need to work together are located together or at least in easy access of each other; and empowering employees to make decisions in the best interest of the customer.

The need to have a "reshipping department" is a good indicator that something is broken in the system. Best practice companies have figured out how to design their processes and organizations properly and are saving money through doing it right the first time.

Helene F Uhlfelder PhD

Good Management Alters The Need To Restructure

In a recent column, I talked about how businesses should organize their processes and their structures around the customer. Most high-performance organizations follow this practice. They also ensure that other support processes, performance feedback mechanisms and cultural factors align to deliver quality products to the customer and a satisfying work environment for the employees. When I work with organizations that continually restructure as a way to improve competitiveness, I tell them, "Changing the structure does not solve all of your problems. In fact, continuous restructuring has negative outcomes if not done appropriately." My advice is based on years of practical experience in hundreds of organizations, not on theory or research.

I have found experts who not only agree with me, but clearly point out some of the negative ramifications of frequent restructuring and how informal structures and networks more closely reflect how work is performed. An article in the fall issue of MIT *Sloan Management Review* reports that in many companies work is completed more by informal networks and cross-department efforts than in the formal, hierarchal structure represented by the "organizational chart." In many companies, reorganizing people and work has produced cost efficiencies, more satisfied customers and higher profits. However, constant restructuring costs money, increases employee skepticism and confusion, and may not be necessary if other aspects of the organization such as process, rewards performance feedback systems and knowledge management systems are in place.

For example, a client hired a consulting firm to complete a study and provide recommendations for the "right" structure needed to enable the organization to meet the fast-changing, time-critical needs of a multitude of customers and stakeholders. The client was sure that the structure and the numbers of employees were the problems. The study uncovered major problems in almost every aspect of the client's operation: lack of standardized processes, minimal use of management information tools, lack of performance feedback (positive or negative), no clear definition of success, lack of information about performance, and managers who had been selected for their technical skill, not their ability to lead and manage people. Incidentally, there were not enough people with the right skills employed. Because the client wanted several structure alternatives from which to choose, the consultant provided four (one was to stay the same). The major outcome of the study was that the structure did not need to change, but most of the process, technology and human systems needed to be improved.

Because the client could not implement all the recommended changes, the decision was made to implement the improvements that represented basic good management practices. This included clearly articulating the organization's and each team's mission, using performance measures across the organization that aligned to their mission and their customer and stakeholder requirements, documenting core processes and roles and responsibilities, increasing cross-organization communication and coaching for all the leaders on communication and team-management skills. Regularly scheduled meetings (using best-practice meeting management skills and tools) were instituted to foster collaboration and cooperation.

What can you do if your organization tends to use frequent restructuring and it's not working? First, step back and ask, "What is the problem we are trying to solve?" Then, look for root causes for the problem. Make sure to examine all possible causes: strategy, clarity, work processes, use of technology, jobs, development, rewards and performance feedback. If there is data to support any of the causes, take a good look at what the data tells you. Next, develop solutions to the core problems, check the solutions for alignment with each other and develop an implementation plan. Make sure the first few steps of the plan are quick wins to demonstrate success early. If restructuring is one of the solutions, make sure you modify processes, rewards, performance feedback and knowledge sharing to support the new structure before you move people. If you are going to spend time and money to restructure, make sure the effort will succeed so you don't have to restructure again in six months.

There's An Art To Restructuring

A client complained, "My organization is about to do another restructuring. Every time we do this, we just change titles and move the same people from one box to another. The end point is that none of our restructuring efforts has produced the results we want. What advice can you give us to make this one different? "

What they were describing is a common practice in many organizations. Very few companies understand why and how to redesign their structure. This tends to result in frustration, turmoil, confusion and resentment.

In order to avoid the negative consequences of restructuring, there are some steps you can take. Remember, there will always be a certain level of anxiety when you ask people to change their group, roles and responsibilities. But these issues can be dealt with effectively with a good change management plan.

First, is restructuring the right solution to the problem?

If an organization has not undertaken a thorough analysis of the business or performance problem it wants to solve, changing the structure may be absolutely the wrong action to take. In fact, the most effective structure redesigns happen after other factors are addressed (e.g., changes to processes, technology or strategic focus). Structure is an enabler of how work is done, not the driver.

If changing the structure is necessary, then there are steps to take to ensure the new structure helps support the business goals. All structures should be based on the organization's strategy, values and principles, the most effective and efficient work processes, and a thorough understanding of customers and products and services.

For example, if the organization's stated strategy is "speed to market," and a key value is "teamwork," then the structure needs to be designed around multiskilled teams who are empowered and enabled to make decisions quickly.

An organization's structure should be designed from the front-line work level to the top of the organization, not from the executive level down. In other words, don't decide that "we need three SVPs and two VPs." Look at the way work should be performed to meet customer requirements and begin defining roles and responsibilities needed to produce the product or service to meet those requirements. As hard as it is, don't think in terms or current jobs or current staff. Think about the right way to do the work and consider who will do the work (and what new skills or competencies are needed) as an implementation issue. Build the structure from the work to the next level of supervision or management. Ask the question, "What leadership, support or management is needed that the team cannot do?" This will help you begin to figure out other levels and support organizations necessary.

Once you have developed all the groups, teams or departments, their roles and responsibilities, and the leadership and support structures needed for success, consider other enabling processes, practices or systems that need to change to make the structure work. This can include new technology, changes to performance-appraisal processes, changes to compensation, or additional training and development. If you leave all these other aspects of the organization the same, the effectiveness of the restructuring will at best be suboptimal and at worse, another failure.

A couple of other pieces of advice: As much as possible, invite the people who will be affected by the change to have some voice in what the new structures will be. These people tend to know more about the day-to-day work, and by involving them, you increase the likelihood of acceptance to the new structure.

Also, develop and execute a change management and communication plan before the new structure is finalized. Make sure key stakeholders understand why the changes are necessary, how they can be involved, and what is in it for them. Restructuring the organization can be a positive thing and can provide competitive advantage if done properly.

Get Rid Of The Walls And Floors

In his book, *The World Is Flat,* Thomas Friedman uses the expression "get rid of the walls and floors" to describe one way you create organizations that are extremely flexible, cost-efficient and competitive in the continuously changing world marketplace. As I was listening to the book on CD, I had a picture of a person free-falling through space and imaged how scary that would be. It hit me that the fear of free-falling is why many organizations and their managers and employees choose not to change from siloed, vertical organizations to wall-less, vertical organizations.

This resistance to change shows up in many ways, such as wanting more data to prove an immediate return on investment.

Even though evidence of the success of horizontal organizations is growing, for some organizations there will never be enough proof. "How can I take out the walls and floors and not kill myself? Won't our profits fall? How do we know that it will work?"

What does it take to make you comfortable enough to jump?

First, it takes a leap of faith. You must believe your organization has the capabilities to survive the fall. This includes having the right processes, systems, people practices and tools in place.

Second, it is critical to have a vision for where you want to be in the future. The vision does not have to be concrete; in fact, you want a dynamic vision that can apply as external conditions change.

Third, your culture needs to reward risk-taking. It's hard to take risks when your success is measured in terms of immediate return on investment.

Fourth, it is extremely useful to have someone "hold your hand." This is not meant in a touchy-feely way, but in the sense of being there with you, coaching you, and providing knowledge and information.

Here is the story of two companies. One organization saw the writing on the wall about the long-term viability of its products and services. Years before the bottom dropped out, a visionary senior VP decided to change the entire manufacturing operation to be lean, process-focused, team-based, measurement-based and fast to change.

Over a four-year period, all processes were examined and either re-engineered or eliminated. Cutting-edge technology was installed to enable new business processes. Everyone was assigned to a team. Organizing around the customer became one of the core principles.

Not only did this organization survive and thrive, eventually it was sold by its owners for a great deal of money. The organization was able to do this because of its visionary leadership, not waiting for 100 percent proof, breaking down traditional departments and developing its people.

The second company also saw its industry changing. Its leaders were more comfortable with gradual change and felt strongly that unless the costs-benefit of any project could be proven ahead of time, no fundamental change would occur. This organization made many small and large improvements to processes, technology, people development, etc.

As the industry changed, the organization could keep up. But it was becoming clear that incremental, cost-reduction-driven projects were not going to help the organization make the type of profit numbers it desired. Every conversation came back to: "Do you have the numbers that prove it? You know we are not risk-takers."

This organization will eventually be forced to tear down walls and floors. Sadly, the competitive advantage of being first or second rather than last will be lost. In its fear of free-falling, this organization will open doors for customers to walk through to get to the competitor.

Recognize Work Boundaries, But Keep Them Fluid

Most people know how important trust is to building and maintaining the many relationships organizations must manage to be successful. This column focuses on a second factor crucial for work relationships: managing the boundaries. Boundary management refers to the interactions, flow of information, and other inputs and outputs at the boundaries in an organization.

This can be the boundaries between suppliers and the organization, between managers and employees, between departments, and between the organization and its customers and stakeholders. In some ways, this is analogous to managing the borders between countries. As in border management, the process can be smooth-flowing or contentious. It can be as difficult as the border between East and West Berlin was during the Cold War or as simple as crossing from Virginia into North Carolina.

There are several components for successful boundary management. One is that the boundaries are clearly understood by all parties. There should be no confusion about where the dividing line is and what the rules are for passage from one side to another. For example, a supplier is clear about the customer's requirements for delivery (e.g., date, quality, method of delivery). Or the finance department knows how the executive team wants to see financial data (e.g., format of graphs, data to include or exclude.) Part of the clarity should include what is acceptable to share such as information and resources. This works best when clear customer requirements are translated into polices and procedures that all people working the boundary are trained in and held accountable for meeting.

The second is that under normal conditions the boundary is fluid and porous, enabling smooth passage, not bottlenecks. By avoiding rigid boundaries between supplier and customer, employee and manager, and various departments, speed of response is enabled. For example, when using an outsource partner, direct communication should be allowed between the organization's manager and personnel and the outsourced personnel. Feedback that must go up the chain of command and not directly to the people involved causes bottlenecks, delays in communication, and confusion. Maintaining flexible job descriptions and allowing the people closest to the work to make day-to-day decisions are other examples of fluid boundaries.

    A third component is measurement, developing and monitoring quantitative and qualitative measures of performance for all involved parties. Some people refer to these as service level agreements (SLAs.) These measures should cover all critical aspects of the work and relationship. Examples include cycle-time requirements, quality requirements, accuracy and timeliness of information and feedback, problem-resolution effectiveness, and teamwork effectiveness.

    A final component of successful relationships pertains to the human and interpersonal capabilities necessary to establish and maintain relationships. This includes people's ability to listen and communicate, handle differences of opinions and resolve conflicts, and utilize tools for effective meetings and group interaction. Critical to the interpersonal factor is having adequate numbers of skilled people to be boundary managers. Maintaining relationships is time-consuming. Asking people who already have more on their plates than they can handle to add this task to their workload guarantees problems in boundary management.

    Jobs must be designed to allow for developing and maintaining regular communication and interaction with a team's suppliers, partners, and internal and external customers. This includes the manager's job: his or her job should include responsibility for making sure the employees have the tools, resources and training
necessary to be successful.

    The manager's role may be 30 percent or more of boundary management: spending time educating stakeholders; acquiring the right education and coaching for the employees;

and having time to provide feedback to employees and suppliers.

So far, we have covered two aspects of relationships and work: trust and boundary management. In future columns, we will examine relationship skill sets and competencies. In the meantime, take this short self-test. On a scale of one to ten, rate trust for each of the relationships your organization has. Then, using the same scale, rate your organization on clarity of boundaries, openness of boundaries, and the level of interpersonal skills for managing boundaries. This will provide you a baseline for your organization's ability to develop and maintain good relationships.

Helene F Uhlfelder PhD

Knowing The Rules Of Partnering Can Pay Off

It's hard to find a company today that does not outsource part of the work it does for its customers. For many organizations, forming alliances is a critical part of the organization's ability to provide quality products and services. As everyone knows who has been involved in creating and managing these outsource relationships, the process is not always smooth nor does it always guarantee that the customer will be happy with the end product or service.

Recently, I had my kitchen remodeled and had some hurricane damage finally repaired. I hired a building and renovation company that I had used before: Their prices were reasonable and the work was performed satisfactorily. The recent project was larger than the first one and required a variety of experts. The contractor could only complete the work by employing subcontractors.

From day one, it was obvious that the various subcontractors did not communicate with each other about their individual portions of the work. The contractor who communicated with each subcontractor one-on-one did not have a master plan that showed everyone how all the work fit together and who had what responsibilities. There was a great deal of frustration, rework and delays. As I told the contractor, "I like dealing with you but the coordination and communication among all the subcontractors leave much to be desired."

Here is another example of what can happen with outsourced relationships. A colleague was engaged as a subcontractor to a large prime contractor on a government contract for an organization with whom he has worked for the past year. My colleague, who is highly conscientious and very customer-focused, has experienced late communications, hostile e-mails and a lack of true partnership with the prime contractor. The prime contractor will not let my colleague talk directly to the client project manager because the prime contractor's organization is bureaucratic and believes in high control. The relationship with the client suffers because there are delays and misunderstanding between the prime and the subcontractor and because there is little direct communication among the parties.

Both of these examples highlight the absence of three very critical aspects of positive outsourced relationships: clear shared expectations, decision-making allowed as close to the work as possible, and regular coordination and communication.

First, it is important when two or more entities decide to work together for there to be clearly articulated expectations and guidelines. Holding team formation sessions at the beginning of the partnership provides an opportunity for everyone to meet each other and develop project ground rules and processes for handling issues. This "pre-work" becomes increasingly critical the more parties involved.

Second, nothing kills self-motivation, ownership of results, and joy in what one does quicker than having responsibility for a job, but not decision-making authority. Best-practice companies allow employees who are closest to the client high levels of decision-making authority (within known limits and guidelines.) If when forming alliances with others you take the time to develop partnership goals, guidelines and boundaries, it is possible to allow front-line people to make decisions in the best interest of the customer. The customer does not care which company has control, they just want the product or service delivered right and on time.

Although last on the list, communication and coordination may be the most important aspect of successful outsourcing or partnering. Regularly scheduled meetings, electronic databases and knowledge management, and a host of other ways to communicate need to be in place early in the relationship and throughout the project. Many times this must be done with little face-to-face communication. Virtual relationships require more attention than those where people actually work together and have time to develop trust.

If you are in an outsourced relationship or a partnership with other organizations, make sure you pay attention to clear shared expectations, decision-making allowed as close to the work as possible, and regular coordination and communication. It will make the difference between a successful one and one that ends in "divorce."

Withholding Information Costs Ultimate Price

Most organizations, both public-sector entities and private companies, rely heavily on outsourced and collaborative relationships to produce products and services for customers. Successful organizations have mastered the politically tricky areas of how to share and manage information and knowledge all sides need to accomplish work. But many organizations still are not sophisticated enough to know that blindly accepting surface information or withholding information will ultimately get them into trouble when dealing with multiple partners and stakeholders. Here are two examples.

Recently I came home from work to find part of my front yard destroyed. After many discussions and phone calls and hearing four different stories, I found out that the project was a joint city/private citizens' project that no one notified me about. The reason I wasn't notified was that one of my neighbors neglected to tell the city engineer that 35 feet of the property she was showing him was on my yard and he did not check the plat (forget the fence that was there).

She had a reason for not telling him it was my yard – resentment about property-line issues. He had reasons for not taking the time to check: He trusted my neighbor's word and didn't want to take the time to research the plat. So, because one woman withheld information and one other person did not take the time to check information, there are negative repercussions and I had to spend hours getting answers.

The second situation involves a client who engaged me to facilitate a task force to redesign a logistics process. Prior to my being hired, another consulting firm (Firm XYZ) had redesigned another related process and thought they would be facilitating this one. When Firm XYZ discovered it would play a supporting role instead, its people were angry. During planning meetings Firm XYZ appeared agreeable and helpful. I explained the process we would use and walked them through all the activities. I would use the materials they had previously developed as the foundation for the work for the new logistics process.

Never once did Firm XYZ tell me that there were problems with the redesigned process they had created. On the first day of the session, when I began facilitating the new task team, it became obvious there were problems. One of their consultants admitted, "Yes, we had this problem before. It is confusing." I asked, "What should we do?" She answered, "I don't know."

On the fly I came up with a solution to keep the task team moving. On the next break, I pulled the XYZ consultant aside and asked, "Why didn't you tell me this before we walked into this in front of the client?"

Her answer was, "Well, the client wanted to use your approach, not mine." Firm XYZ withheld information because they felt they had lost work that should have been rightfully theirs and they were going to passive-aggressively show that what I did was not as good as what they could have done. Instead, this was costing the client time and money.

Both stories are examples of how important it is to make sure that in any type of partnership or collaborative business relationship there is full disclosure and full fact-checking. No matter how honest and truthful people believe and say they are, we are all human. For a variety of reasons, people may unintentionally "forget" to tell you all the facts. This is why it is extremely important to have checklists and planning meetings. The other thing important to remember is that if you think you can win by making someone else look bad or suffer, it usually backfires.

My client called me after the terrible meeting and said, "I still can't understand why Firm XYZ did what they did. Don't they understand how bad that looks to us, the client?"

Measurement Can Be A Four-letter Word

While talking with a client about an upcoming software implementation, I asked the project sponsor, "What are the business reasons for this implementation and what critical business measures are you hoping to impact?" He was able to answer the first question, but could not identify what scorecard measures the organization hoped to improve with the new information system.

He went on to explain that his company, a $1 billion operation, did not have any scorecards that the executives used for managing the business. They each reviewed multitudes of numbers, often different ones that depended on a person's individual preference.

This organization is not alone. During the startup phase of every project, I ask project sponsors and executive level leaders, "Do you have a scorecard that you use to manage the business? What are the critical measures that you include? Is the scorecard balanced or are there only financial measures utilized?"

Thirty percent of the companies do not use scorecards. Between sixty and seventy percent use such measures at the leadership and executive level but do not share the information company-wide. Of that group, maybe half have a balanced scorecard that includes financial, customer, employee and other measures. Maybe twenty percent of the companies to which I talked have a balanced scorecard that is utilized throughout the organization.

This phenomenon is puzzling and troubling as it is generally known that organizations that utilize balanced scorecards and expect their people to use them to run the business outperform organizations that do not utilize such metrics. For example, one organization was able to transform a bankruptcy into a growth opportunity by creating and executing scorecards, by teaching every worker the basics of finance, graphing and problem solving, and by requiring daily meetings where everyone reviewed progress and discussed how to improve the critical numbers.

Another that did not utilize any type of measurement system found itself continually losing money and undertook a drastic cost-cutting campaign that left the organization demoralized, short-staffed and barely able to conduct its business. The people in this second outfit had no idea how bad things were as the financial figures were only shared with a few top executives.

If it is so obvious that using scorecards is a positive practice, why do so many organizations avoid this approach to managing business? One of the reasons is that many people do not like to be measured. Most employees have experienced measurement used as a way to punish people, not as a way for continuous improvement. Measures may have been used to pit people against each other and create conflicts within the organization.

Another reason is that many professionals do not believe there is a way to measure their work. They believe that being able to measure creativity, quality or customer satisfaction only applies in manufacturing. A third reason is that it takes time, resources, training and tools for scorecards to work. Many companies falsely believe the cost outweighs the benefits because they have not seen results from past efforts. Lastly, sharing measures openly throughout an organization requires trust, cooperation and participation. If an organization's climate is one of competition, secrecy, power and control, sharing scorecard information runs counter to the culture

If you truly want an organization that demonstrates high performance, productivity, and customer and employee satisfaction, consider developing and utilizing scorecards. The process must start with senior leadership's identifying the overall critical measures for the business ensuring a balance between the types of measures used.

The process must include training and coaching for people to understand and effectively use the information. Often, the process must include changes to the way information is captured and distributed. However, sometimes the most effective measures are those that require no fancy technology, just some paper and a pen and a commitment to manage the business on data and facts, not just hunches.

Helene F Uhlfelder PhD

Here's A Script That Wins Applause

Recently I spent a week traveling with my actor grandson on the bus with a New York theater company's production of "The Music Man" and was reminded of what teams can accomplish even in the worst of circumstances.

The 50-plus actors and actresses, production personnel and musicians range in age between 9 and 76 years old, travel across North America and perform on a different stage four out of five nights often after a four- to seven-hour bus trip. Each stop on the tour involves rapid adjustment to different venues and stages, changes in hotel accommodations, and inconsistent eating and sleeping schedules. In spite of these challenges, each day and/or night, the company delivers a performance that brings the audience to their feet clapping and cheering by the end of the play.

I wondered if there aren't some lessons about teamwork that can be learned from this amazing group of people. I believe there are some core principles that apply not only to performers, but to all types of teams.

First, the group shares a common purpose — to provide a high-quality, high-value entertainment experience for audiences. I never saw a "mission" statement, but I bet if I had polled the company members, they would have all made similar comments about their purpose.

Second, they practiced working together before they went on the road. They practiced their craft in pairs, as individuals and as a full company. They got to know each other in a variety of circumstances before having to appear on stage to a paying audience.

Third, they were given constant feedback about their performance in the beginning of and throughout the tour. When they did something well, they were told, and they received corrective feedback in order to improve their performance. As actors and musicians, they expect this type of feedback and would have found it strange not to be provided direction.

Fourth, they were flexible when change was needed. I did not hear anyone complain about having to perform an act or dance differently because the stage was too short or because an understudy was in a role because the other actor was sick. In fact, when changes were announced each evening two hours before the show, people merely asked clarifying questions. Fifth, people supported each other without being asked. If one actor forgot a line or missed a cue, another actor seamlessly adjusted so the audience had no idea a mistake had been made. Finally, there was a great deal of positive reinforcement for a job well done. Yes, the audience may have clapped a little more for the two leads and the two children, but the whole troop received booming rounds of applause.

Two critical enabling processes helped ensure the company's success: hiring and organizing. The people who recruited, interviewed and hired the various individuals had to have been consciously aware of the key traits and capabilities necessary for the work. All the actors had to be able to sing, dance and either play or be able to learn a musical instrument. For several roles, people had to be a certain height and weight. The audition process had screened people for temperament, tolerance for uncertainty and ability to work strange hours. There were no prima donnas or rigid personalities in the group.

Without great organization and people's abiding by the rules, the company would have never made it out of New York. Everyone knew the schedule, where they sat on the bus, when they had time to eat and what would happen to them if they were late. Everyone was expected to check the updated binder each day and was held accountable for knowing any schedule changes. No one was ever late. No one missed the bus.

Could your teams meet a challenge such as this? Has your organization done its job in providing the foundations for outstanding team performance? If the answer is "no," it may be time to get your team's show on the road to better performance by implementing the practices previously described you might even get some applause.

Helene F Uhlfelder PhD

The Dance Became A Business Lesson

There are lessons about managing an organization that can be found in the most unusual places. Recently I had the pleasure of attending, and participating in, a performance by the Nederlands Dans Theater II that was part of the Virginia Arts Festival. The dancers --and directors, advisers, musicians, technicians and costumers-- are a fine-tuned team of exceptional performers that achieve their mission and goals beautifully and seamlessly. They exemplify a true high-performance organization of fifty people who have perfected their products and services to delight the customer.

Imagine introducing twelve new, untrained people into a tight working group of twelve performers. And expecting the novices to be able to integrate into the team without any training, instruction or advance planning. Could your organization manage this without high levels of disruption and possible loss of productivity or quality? Probably not, but the dance troop accomplished this feat by applying three management practices all organizations talk about but rarely achieve: involvement, leadership and teamwork.

History, practice and research have demonstrated that when employees and customers are involved in how work gets done and how final products and services are designed; there are much higher levels of employee and customer satisfaction. The dancers must have known this.

They went into the audience and selected people randomly to go with them to the stage. Without any verbal instruction, the audience members began dancing and moving with their partners. There was an immediate, positive response from the rest of the audience (the customers) and expressions of delight from the audience participants. The professional dancers, through a variety of nonverbal cues, were involved as a team leading the newcomers through the routines.

Common Sense Advice

How do you take twelve novices and quickly provide them direction? The answer in this case was through leadership. Each professional dancer was responsible for quickly ascertaining what the audience member could do, then, without any words, leading them through ten minutes of performing. The leadership the dancers provided was through eye contact, hand gestures and subtle movements. What made this possible was that the "leader" knew his/her job and focused on providing the exact cues and reinforcement to enable the newcomer to perform. Although there appeared to be a "lead" dancer, all the dancers served as leaders during the time twenty-four people were on stage. There were no squabbles or power struggles. There wasn't time; the focus was on performing.

Without any agendas and team meetings, twenty-four people who had never worked together before became a high-performance team through practical teamwork. As one of the audience members thrust into this new "job," I had to apply teaming best practices if I was going to help the team continue to look good. This included watching my leader, paying attention to the other people dancing around me (listening and watching), following the cues provided by the various dancers, and supporting others in whatever way I could (like getting out of the way or moving to where someone pointed).

All of us were focused on the team doing well, not on who could look better or on competing with each other. The newcomers quickly learned how to adjust what we did, just like the dancers had shown us. We must have done OK because we got loud applause, and one woman later asked me, "Did you all rehearse that ahead of time?"

If twenty-four people can be a high-performance team in less than ten minutes, your organization can too. Remember to plan as many involvement events as possible for your employees and your customers. Allow and encourage formal and informal leadership from all levels of the organization. And do everything you can to foster teamwork: Remove boundaries, provide time and space for teaming, and build fun into the work of running your business.

What a wonderful thing it would be if people left work each day feeling they had been part of something special.

Does Your Organization Give And Take Feedback?

Everyone claims they have been trained in communication and feedback skills. Unfortunately, no one is as good at these skills as they think they are.

Furthermore, the organization's culture heavily influences whether people use these skills or not. For example, where one company's culture was "polite and genteel," people did not say things directly that might upset someone else. In another organization, the managers told me that they did not believe in empathizing with people on certain issues because "sounding empathetic makes you look weak."

The way an organization uses feedback and communication tells you a great deal about its culture. These skills are vital for the organization to achieve its goals. It's not about being nice; it's about being successful.

If you want your organization to use feedback and communication effectively, there are eight principles to consider:

1. Real, active listening is important and valuable. People must see value in the time and effort it takes to learn to do this and to practice doing it. Feedback needs to provide something beneficial to the person giving it and/or receiving it.

2. Other people have a right to their own opinions and feelings. Although this statement may sound simplistic, many people have a tough time accepting the fact that other people may think or feel differently than they do this does not mean people can behave any way they wish. There are still norms and standards for how people act toward each other in a work environment. It is the respect for the other person's right to feel and think what they wish that is critical.

3. Listening for and understanding facts and feelings are equally important. There is a tendency for us to accept facts more readily than how someone feels. If people are uncomfortable with human emotion, they will not be effective listeners and communicators. To be able to provide feedback to others, we must be able to hear and understand both what the facts are and how the person feels about the facts.

4. Demonstrating empathy is critical. Empathy is the ability to stand in someone else's shoes and understand how it must feel to be there. It is not sympathy. It is also not the same as agreeing with the other person. The ability to demonstrate empathy is one of the most critical skills a manager, leader or team member can have; it is very powerful. Saying you understand how someone else feels is not the same as demonstrating it. It may mean having to listen to and demonstrate empathy for more than one sentence.

5. Honesty is not the same as saying anything you want to say. Honesty in communication involves saying things because they are true and need to be communicated for a positive reason. The key point is to communicate in a way that demonstrates respect for the other person.

6. Trust and relationship need to be in place. It is much easier to hear from or give feedback to someone with whom we have established a relationship. When we know the person, have some shared history, and they trust we are giving them feedback for good, positive reasons, the process is easier.

7. Corrective feedback needs to be balanced with positive feedback. Studies also have shown that the best and quickest way to teach someone a new behavior is through both positive reinforcement and corrective feedback. But there needs to be a balance of positive feedback. In fact, studies have shown that it is best to give four positive feedback statements for every one negative.

8. Training, practice, reinforcement and modeling increase the likelihood of people giving feedback. People must use the skills after training and see their managers provide feedback. Giving feedback is a competency that develops when people see other people doing it and being reinforced for doing it.

One of the signs of a high-performance organization is the ability of people to give and receive feedback. Can your organization do this? If not, you may be missing a valuable way to improve organization performance.

Helene F Uhlfelder PhD

A Lesson In How To Make A Great Leader

A very successful local businessman, Steve, sat next to me at a holiday dinner party given by some close friends. We got into a discussion about what he thinks contributed to his success and what he thinks it means to be a leader. His story provides real-world examples of what it takes to be a successful businessperson and a good leader.

The most critical event that began Steve's journey happened more than twenty years ago and was a conversation he had with his boss, Jeffrey. Steve was running one of Jeffery's businesses and believed he was doing an excellent job. Steve was bright, energetic, aggressive and highly motivated to succeed. One day Jeffery asked to speak to Steve. Steve was sure that Jeffery was going to tell him what a wonderful job he was doing. Instead, Jeffery told Steve that some of his leadership behavior was unacceptable and that if Steve did not change, Steve would never be successful or get to continue managing Jeffery's business.

Steve was devastated, but listened to the feedback. He heard that he had to be less aggressive with his employees, that he needed to listen to people more, and that he had to demonstrate, not just espouse, behaviors such as allowing his employees to make more decisions on their own. Because Steve respected Jeffery so much and because Jeffery had been coaching him on how to be successful, Steve listened and began to change.

Over the next few years, Steve continuously sought out opportunities to learn and practice being a good leader. He had decided that one core truth to being successful was to create and maintain a good relationship with customers. He made sure that every employee from the lowest paid person to the most senior executives understood that the relationship with the customer is everyone's responsibility. Steve created a culture that said that all customers are greeted and treated with respect. To work at Steve's company, all employees had to smile at, be pleasant to and offer to assist customers. They were taught to respond quickly and happily to complaints and fix problems without causing the customer any additional duress.

Steve's business grew and prospered. Although other businesses like his drew customers from a local radius, his customers came from every place. People would drive farther to deal with Steve's company than any other similar business.

As Steve's company became more successful, Steve realized that he could not make all the decisions anymore and that he had to allow other people more decision-making responsibility. Even though he was afraid that the business would suffer, he began training and mentoring his managers and employees to make wise decisions. Not only did the business not suffer, it prospered even more.

As I reflected on Steve's story, it became evident that three key lessons can be learned. One is that providing a person with honest, direct corrective feedback can make a difference. The stronger the existing relation is between the two people, the more likely it is that the feedback, though difficult to hear, will be more readily received. Had no one told Steve about his unacceptable behavior, Steve would have continued to act the same way and probably not been as successful as he is.

Second, customer (and employee) relationships make or break the business. People will drive miles to deal with a company that shows them respect and appreciation for their continued business. The focus on relationship, not the sell, produces more sales and revenue.

Third, no one person can make all the decisions in a company. It causes bottlenecks, and it frustrates employees and customers. The closer decision-making can be to the people who deal with customers, the better.

One last point: Steve continues to try and improve his leadership skills. He, like the rest of us, can always improve in some way. A good leader knows that. What areas can you improve upon?

Helene F Uhlfelder PhD

Resolve Conflict By Process Improvement

Seventy-five to eighty-five percent of the conflicts in organizations are due to problems related to factors other than personal differences. A large majority of these conflicts are due to poorly defined or seriously broken work processes. Because the root cause of the conflicts is process-related, standard conflict resolution techniques can only provide temporary relief from the conflict.

A more effective means of and a less threatening approach to resolving conflicts is the use of process mapping and process improvement tools. For example, one of my clients decided that the conflict between various groups involved in a complicated process had to be resolved as these conflicts were causing rework, customer dissatisfaction, continuous distraction and wasted time and energy. The people in the various groups had been trained in problem-solving and conflict-resolution techniques and had used them to try to resolve the problems, but nothing had worked. I suggested that they do a process summit where all the involved groups and stakeholders would be in the room and that we use process-mapping and process-improvement tools to identify and fix the process. In other words, focus on the process rather than on the people.

This was arranged, and thirty people attended. The approach we used started with everyone understanding the current process (the process was documented before the session). To avoid subjective decision-making, we used measures and data to understand the current process and its failings. Before looking at the problems and variances within the process, we analyzed the inputs to the process to understand the issues, inaccuracies and problems that occurred before the people in the room began working on their steps of the process. We also looked at the process from the customers' viewpoints. How well was the present process delivering a product or service to the customers? How high was the customers' satisfaction or dissatisfaction with what they received?

The next part in the approach involved looking at each step in the process and each transition in the process to identify variances and root causes for those variances. We examined the impact of technology-enabled vs. manual steps. We looked at skills and knowledge, communication, decision-making and other factors at each step so that all root causes could be considered before development of solutions. We used the 80-20 rule to determine which root causes, if corrected or alleviated, would fix 80 percent of the problems. Lastly, the group, through use of a consensus-building problem-solving method, agreed upon solutions and developed an action plan. Where appropriate, this included changes to the process itself (adding or deleting steps), improvements to educating customers, use of automated tools and clear definition of roles and responsibilities.

At the end of the day, everyone in the room had a much clearer understanding of why the conflicts were occurring, solutions that could be implemented over the next few months and a clear action plan to hold themselves accountable. Although never mentioned directly, all the "conflicts" were aired in a non-accusing, non-threatening manner.

There were some factors that made this session go smoothly. One was that the people in the room had been using team skills and scorecards and had been trained and coached in how to use team decision-making skills prior to the process summit. A second factor was that they engaged a neutral, assertive facilitator who kept the session focused and positive. The facilitator also knew all of the players and was familiar with the work the various groups did. A third factor was that members of the leadership team were in the room and actively involved. This was critical for several reasons: fast decision-making and demonstrated commitment to fixing the problems.

The next time your organization faces conflicts among groups, ask yourself: Would a session focused on process improvement be the right approach to resolve this conflict? If the answer is "yes," you can follow the steps outlined in this column to both fix the process and decrease the conflict.

Helene F Uhlfelder PhD

Saying Thank You Improves Performance

While watching television recently, I saw a commercial that used saying thank you as a way to promote the company's products and services. Ironically, I have spent the past few weeks training and coaching an organization's managers and associates on the basics of behavior change including the power of consequences. If you want to help change any type of behavior, there are only two things you need to understand: antecedents to behavior – cues or triggers – and consequences of behavior – things that occur after a particular behavior happens that reinforce, punish or ignore the behavior. In behavioral science terms, saying thank you is a type of consequence – positive reinforcement.

Before sharing some examples of how positive reinforcement has helped improve organizations' performance, I will explain some basic concepts. Antecedents are cues or triggers that prompt people to do something. A red light is an antecedent for stopping at a traffic light. A weather forecast for rain is a cue to close your car windows before you leave the car in the parking lot at work. Job descriptions are cues for how to perform your job. Consequences are things that happen after a particular behavior has occurred. Getting a ticket after running a red light is a consequence that is meant to punish the act of running a red light. Getting an A on a test is a consequence for studying and answering test questions correctly. The A is positive reinforcement for desirable behaviors such as studying.

When most companies want to improve performance, they tend to focus all their attention on the antecedents: provide more training, tell people to work harder, etc. However, after years of theoretical study and practical application, researchers have learned that consequences have four times the impact on behavior that antecedents have. Saying thank you for a job well done is going to improve performance much more than rewriting work policies.

Although there are several types of consequences – positive reinforcement, punishment and neutral – this column will cover only positive reinforcement. For positive reinforcement to be most effective it needs to be specific, immediate, proportional and personal – the acronym SIPP is a helpful reminder. Here is an example of a good positive reinforcement statement. Just after Sam offers to help Harold, say, "Sam, thank you for offering to help Harold with the spreadsheet for this week's numbers." Waiting three months to thank Sam is too long, and providing Sam a $200 bonus is out of proportion to the act. Saying "thanks for your help" is not specific enough for the person to know for what exactly you are reinforcing her or him.

There are two more important things to know about positive reinforcement. For consequences to be considered positive, the person receiving the consequence must see the consequence as positive. For example, if I hate speaking in front of a group of people and my manager rewards me for high performance by telling me I get to speak at the next all-hands meeting, I am not positively reinforced. I am being punished. Remember, just because a consequence appears positive to you, it may not be positive to the other person. The second thing to remember is that you must be sincere when you deliver positive reinforcement. Many people feel that giving too much positive reinforcement is fake and artificial. They are correct if the person delivering the reinforcement does not really mean it. Sincere, immediate positive feedback is always appreciated.

Here are examples of how correctly provided positive reinforcement helped organizations improve performance:

- Thanking people for arriving on time to a meeting and starting the meeting on time reinforced on-time behavior and all teams reported an improvement in meeting efficiency.

- Hand-written notes from an executive to front-line employees for suggestions on how to improve processes resulted in an increase in associates' suggestions for process improvements.

- Spot rewards of a dinner for four given to people who found small ways to reduce costs resulted in overall cost savings.

A pat on the back, a letter of appreciation and a sincere thank you for a job well done can make the difference between average and high performance.

Thank you for reading this column.

When Public Conflict Swamps Your Boat

Years ago, I took an eighteen-day raft and kayak trip down the Colorado River through the Grand Canyon on a private permit with sixteen friends. All of us were skilled whitewater rafters, and many of us had been the lead paddler in a raft.

We decided that each day a different person would be the raft leader, which meant this person told the paddling team which way to steer the boat, which people should paddle harder and which strokes should be used. I was selected to be the raft leader just before we hit the first difficult rapid. As we approached the first wave, I yelled, "Draw right." Immediately, a discussion took place among several people. "I think we should go more left." "No, we need to stay more in the middle."

As a result of the conflicting opinions, we were all paddling in different directions, and the boat flipped over, dumping us into the fifty-four degree water. Once we righted the raft and all of us were back in our places, we had to renegotiate the rules. We decided that there was to be no conflict or second opinions voiced while we were in a rapid. Any conflicts over how we should have run the rapid would be handled when we were in flat water.

I was reminded of this incident as I observed a team of people attempting to come to closure on a solution to a problem the team had in providing their customers with timely and accurate information. Two team members began arguing about whether one person should have resent some critical information to the other person or not. Person A had requested Person B to resend an e-mail to her with updated financial information. Person B said, "I sent that to you once, and I am not sending it again. It takes too much of my time to always resend information to you just because you are too disorganized to find your own information." The interchange grew more and more heated until I was able to get both people to stop talking. (They were talking so loud that they could not hear me say, "Time out. Let's take this off-line.")

Although no one was thrown into a dangerous rapid, the effects and consequences of this public disagreement were negative and strong. The original problem was not solved; trust among team members decreased; team productivity was reduced; and outside parties became involved, distracting additional people from other critical job duties.

What should have occurred in this situation to avoid the negative outcomes? First, the two people should have used a few basic listening and communication skills such as rephrasing and empathy statements (such as, "I understand it is frustrating to you to have to resend information. I hear you telling me that it takes extra time, and you think I do this too much of the time.")

Second, if listening and acknowledging the other person's viewpoint did not work, one of the two people should have suggested that they schedule a time to discuss this issue outside of the meeting (such as, "It appears we have a strong difference of opinion on this subject. Let's talk after the meeting about this.") Lastly, the team leader should have spoken up and taken charge of the situation. If necessary, the leader could have stood up and commanded the two people to stop talking, called for a break and talked to each of the individuals during the break.

In almost every organization with which I have worked, people are extremely uncomfortable dealing directly with conflict. When conflict occurs in public and is ignored or mishandled, people's fears about conflict resolution are increased. The best time to prepare people for dealing with conflict is when the situation is calm, and people can, in a safe environment, practice the skills necessary to use later in real situations. Like those of us who were in the raft, people are more open to negotiation in calm water.

I've Never Seen So Many Men Shopping

Today, everyone bemoans the death of customer service and quality – in everything from kitchen remodeling to computer help. So it was delightful to recently experience how true customer service and quality pays off for a business.

A local fine-menswear store announced it was closing one of its stores and was marking all the merchandise down to sell it quickly. Past customers were sent a letter and invited to shop before the sales announcement was made to the public. When the doors opened at 9 a.m., there were twenty of us in line: nineteen men and me. By the time I reached the forty-four longs and grabbed five sports jackets, fifty more people were in the store – forty-seven men and three women. I realized I have never in my life seen that many men shopping at one time. As I stood in line waiting to pay for the two sports jackets I was buying, twenty people were lined up behind me, waiting to check out. I have never seen that many men standing patiently in line to pay for armloads of clothes.

The point of this story is to illustrate how businesses can use high quality and exceptional customer service to sell products, even products that are more costly and that ultimately produce more bottom-line profits for the business. There are several components to the equation for success: reputation, consistency, personal customer service, high quality products and extra touches.

This store's reputation (and brand) was formed over the years, and everyone who shopped there knew the store as "one of the best men's clothing stores in the area." Everything they did reinforced this reputation (knowledgeable sales staff, products that held their value, the shopping bags they used, and a myriad of other factors). Their reputation would not have remained good if not for the second factor, consistency. Whenever you went into the store, the message and merchandise were consistent. How you were treated did not depend on who was working that day. You did not have to worry, "Will the jacket fall apart after three cleanings?" You knew it would not. For decades, people expected and received the same high-quality attention and products.

While in the store, I watched how certain customers were treated. You could tell that the sales staff knew these customers' sizes, tastes, and budget. Many companies provide exceptional customer service to their high-profit customers. However, that day, even though the staff didn't know me personally, one of them offered to help me, carried clothes to the front of the store, and provided me the same attention that the high-dollar spenders received.

Normally, one part of good customer service is to have an easy return or exchange policy. For this sale there was a large sign posted that said, "All sales are final." Normally for me to spend money on higher-priced items, I need reassurance that my husband can bring the garments back in case they don't work. However, I was not worried for one reason: This store only carries high-quality products. I didn't have to worry that the garments might be flawed. In addition, I knew that the store would provide tailoring, and good men's garments allow for alterations for size adjustments (quality and customer service combined).

Lastly, it's the extra touches that add to the reputation, customer service and repeat business. Here's an example: I was asked did I want them to keep the clothes I bought at the store so it would be more convenient for my husband to come in and get his coats and pants altered. Another example was when the staff observed that the checkout line was very long, they gathered more staff at the counter to share tasks like handling the billing, wrapping the clothes, and running back and forth to get different sizes for the customers so they wouldn't lose their place in the checkout line.

The lesson learned was that every business is capable of increasing profits by focusing on quality and customer service. If you can get men to stand in line to shop, you can do anything.

Reversing A Nosedive

Logically it would seem that companies that know they are in financial trouble would try to do as much as they can to keep their customers. Even when a company needs to implement cost-cutting measures, customers should be the group least impacted because they impact revenue growth or decline. Recently, I experienced a company that provides great examples of how to do everything wrong. Its mistakes can be a lesson for other companies trying to recover financially and keep its customers.

Lately I have been forced to fly "Nameless" airline for business purposes. After several weeks of late arrivals and lost bags, I decided to ask various "Nameless" employees why each of the various problems happen. Their answers provide real-life examples of broken processes, too much centralized decision-making, too much outsourcing, technology that is fractured and not integrated, and dissatisfied employees. The most frequent excuse I heard was, "We have no control over this. Someone else manages and controls this process or issue."

To help you avoid these same problems, here is what the company does wrong and what could be done to fix the problems.

First there are the broken processes. When a bag is "mishandled" and can't be found, the processes for reporting the loss, for being kept informed about the status of the bag, and for receiving compensation are dispersed among various departments and outsourced companies. First, you must stand in line to report the lost item. No one can say for sure where the bag is or when the status of the bag will be updated. One of the "Nameless" employees explained to me that mishandled bags happen every week and countless times. I was told people have repeatedly complained about this, and no action is currently being undertaken to fix the problem. The airport counter people provide you with a lost baggage identity number and a phone number to call.

The phone number takes you to an automated system that

can only be updated by the personnel at the destination airport, so no one really knows where the bag is until its arrives and is entered into the computer system. If you want to talk to a human being, you have to dig through the company's Web site. The call center personnel do not have any more information than you do, and their common answer to most questions was, "We do not control that. We are not responsible for that." It appears there is no one information database that is kept updated.

When a problem occurred that could be easily handled by one of the employees, such as finding alternative ways to get you to your destination or being flexible about how to compensate you for lost luggage, it becomes obvious that no front-line employees are given the right to make decisions. The stock answer for a request to change how they handle a problem was, "I can't make that decision. I will be glad to refer you to the appropriate person who you can call or e-mail when you get to your destination."

Finally, almost every employee I dealt with was as frustrated as I was. This showed in their attitudes and actions. Most employees were short-tempered and rude. Even when they said, "I understand your problem," their tone of voice and curtness undermined any positive words they verbalized.

Here are three solutions for fixing similar problems:

1. If money is tight and you need to cut corners and adjust your processes, fix the customer-facing processes first.

2. If you are going to be reliant on technology-enabled processes, fix the systems that provide customer information first and make sure the front-line people dealing with the customer have the most current, accurate information.

3. Take care of your employees in whatever ways you can

afford. This should be the place that extra time and effort are spent. Your employees directly impact customers and represent your organization.

None of this is easy, but if you don't fix the customer-facing processes, you'll continue to lose money and goodwill.

Helene F Uhlfelder PhD

Remove The Emotion When Change Is Afoot

One day I spent fourty-five minutes on hold waiting for technical help for a digital camera. Every two minutes a recorded voice said, "Your call is important to us. Please hold for the next available technician." I finally gave up and hung up the phone. I swore that I would never buy another product from that manufacturer.

Another day, I tried to talk to someone about a new credit card I received that had my first name spelled wrong. After listening to all the response choices and finding that none fit this problem, I pushed a button that sounded close to what the problem was.

This ended up being the wrong thing to do because the next levels of choices were not even close, and there was no way to get back to an operator. I hung up and redialed the original number, listened carefully, and pushed "0" for an operator. After twenty minutes of waiting, I hung up. My card, which I promise I will never use, still has "Helena" as my first name.

Each on of us has stories such as these. So, where are all the people who are supposed to be handling these calls? My suspicion is that they all come to work at 4 p.m. to 7 p.m. during the week, while normal people eat dinner, and 9:30 a.m. on Saturdays and Sundays (yes, people really do call on these days). This is when people call to sell you insurance or telephone services, want you to donate to the firefighters, police officers or wildlife fund, or answer a few marketing research questions.

In a massive movement to cut costs and make processes more efficient, companies invented call centers. The idea was that though the use of technology, a central call center could handle a variety of customer and technical issues.

Companies could even delegate this work to another business across the country or half a world away. Ironically, the person closest to the customer is now often not even an employee of the company who made the product or sold you the service. This is the new definition of customer service? I can list you products or services I will not use again because of how I was handled or avoided on the phone.

Not all call centers are bad. Some companies realized that unhappy customers can be made into happy ones by quickly handling their complaints or problems. Some companies have skilled operators that answer on the second ring and fix your problem immediately. You can tell that these companies not only centralized operations and designed good customer-relations systems, but they also trained their people and staffed adequately to handle the calls they get.

There are ways to reap the benefits of technology and centralization and still provide excellent customer service. Such solutions start with the company's values and mission and permeate how work processes are designed and how people are organized, developed and rewarded. Businesses can be designed to deliver excellent customer service by always asking these questions
:   How will this impact our customers? Will this make us more or less customer focused? Are we making it easier or harder for customers to do business with us? Are we using technology to be a "cheap and dirty" company or as a way to empower our workers and collaborate more with our suppliers and customers? If your answers don't support a true customer-centric philosophy, think twice about the price your company will pay when customers have problems and there is no one there to fix them.

And then there's the duck. I wish I could remember the company that did this, but I can't. If you had a question or a problem, there was an 800 number to call. Prompts one to six were the usual: "If you wish to order, press one," "If you wish to speak to a customer representative, press two, "and so on.

The last prompt was, "If you want to hear a duck quack, press seven." A real duck quacked; you laughed; and you went back to the other options with a smile on your lips. It made me realize that a short wait for a human did not have to be boring, and a little humor helped me be more tolerant.

Common Sense Advice

Innovative Companies Just Don't Happen, They're Created

Google is known both for its high stock price and its very innovative practices. TIME Magazine's recent cover story described the lengths the company goes to hire, retain, motivate and stimulate employees to produce innovative products and services. Ironically, this same week, I spent two days with a government support contracting organization, USCo, which, although very profitable today, is facing the challenge of how to invent, develop, and sell new products and services in the future to continue its fifteen to twenty percent year-to-year revenue growth for the next five years with the current products and services.

USCo's senior leadership team had convened for a two-day session to refine its new organization structure and agree upon final details for how the organizational dynamics will work. The other objective was to decide what new business to explore based on future market trends. As this was the first time all met face-to-face as a team, there was little overt disagreement and open discussion. On the new structure, topics were superficially discussed, and agreement reached.

When time came to brainstorm new products and services, the group continually reverted to the same products and services they provide today. They could not envision anything new. When pushed and challenged with new ideas, new markets and new customers, they grew resistant and defensive. It was obvious, even to them, that they all had the same experiences, same backgrounds, thought alike and had the same comfort zones. And, as one person commented, "We won't be able to achieve our five-year targets if we don't change our mindsets and get out of our boxes."

This really isn't surprising. USCo, like so many governments support contractors, hires its employees mainly from the former branches of the military. Eighty percent of these employees go straight from active service to working on projects similar to those they did in the service. Their clients are a government agency or a branch of the service, and the employer is private industry, so very little has changed. The employee will have had little new training other than orientation training to the new company, will get little exposure to people with diverse ideas, and will end up working with people who think very much alike.

Contrast these practices with what Google does. First, some of their hiring practices screen for the truly unique. Would you know this is an advertisement for a job: "First 10-digit prime found in consecutive digits of e.com"? Google allows people to spend ten percent of their time on pursuit of far-out ideas. People have space and equipment to play at work. Anyone in the company can schedule time to plan and present his or her new ideas to a panel for consideration for development, although they must come with a business plan. Because retaining bright, young engineers is priority #1, Google provides many fringe benefits, such as professional and personal development opportunities.

Your organization is probably not one of the extremes mentioned here. Wherever you are in the continuum, there are steps you can take to create a culture of innovation:

> 1. Hire people with diversity of thought, ideas, background and experience. This means hiring non-military people as well as former military for defense contractors.
>
> 2. Provide formal and informal settings for them to meet, talk, work and present. Traditional cubicle space isn't conducive for creative thought.
>
> 3. Reward success and trying. Google doesn't reward people for success. It's OK to come up with ideas that bomb. The requirement to have a business case is a critical one because it makes people think about the financial side as well as the creative side.

4. Provide continuous professional development to include skills that help with team creativity and problem-solving. People who have not been exposed to how to think creatively or how to work as a team need to be taught these skills. It won't happen without help and guidance.

Helene F Uhlfelder PhD

Why I Bought Another Handbag

I travel to client sites most weeks, which forces me to frequently fly and stay in hotels. Each hotel and airline provides customer feedback cards, supposedly to acquire "valuable customer feedback to help improve customer service." Because I believe businesses cannot change if they do not receive immediate, specific feedback, I complete many of these cards, mostly when I have experienced bad or less than promised services. I have not received a response from any of the hotels or airlines that I have written, and I am a preferred customer in most of these cases. Even when I provide feedback face-to-face, particularly with airlines, my issues are generally not resolved to my satisfaction, and the personnel do not appear to care.

Imagine my surprise when I had a positive experience in a situation with a store when I had a problem. For several weeks I walked past the store's display window and noticed an unusual handbag. I loved it, but it was costly so I passed by the store. One day, I walked by the display and decided to go in and purchase the bag. The sales staff assured me that the bag would hold up well, and if it got dirty, I could wipe it clean with a wet cloth.

I was delighted. People stopped me on the street, in grocery stores and going up elevators to tell me how much they loved the bag. As with any article I own, it eventually goes on the road with me. For several weeks I took it every place: on airplanes, to client sites and to run errands. It started getting dirty, very dirty, so I tried wiping it with a damp cloth. That only made it worse: It had watermarks in addition to black marks.

My granddaughter convinced me to take it back to the store and tell them about the bag. I agreed to do this and showed the bag to the salesperson. At first, she told me that the bag was meant for "occasional" use and that I should have never been told that it was durable and cleanable by anything once it was that dirty. After reasserting my displeasure with the bag and repeating how much I loved it, the woman said, "Would you be happy if we gave you a new bag like this?" I was floored and immediately said, "Yes."

As I was waiting for them to get a new bag from the storage area, I mentioned that I did need a bag that could stand up to my life- style, if this bag could not.

She said, "I think we have the exact bag you need for this." She was right, so I bought it.

> 1. Don't ask for customer feedback if you are not going to use the information to improve the customer experience or customer service.
>
> 2. When a customer takes the time to fill out the comment card or give you personal feedback, at least acknowledge the comments and thank the person for taking the time to provide you useful information.
>
> 3. Be mindful of the fact that poor response to the customer will probably result in the customer not doing business with you again, which translates into less profits for you.
>
> 4. If you make the customer happy and respond to delight the customer, the customer will continue to do business with you, and like in the case with the handbag, the customer will be willing to spend a little more knowing you stand by your products and services.

I love both of my handbags and have told many people about my experience with this store. This is the last advantage of excellent customer service: free marketing.

Helene F Uhlfelder PhD

What A Difference A Human Being Makes

In these days of self-service, when the assumption is that pressing numbers on a telephone or sending an e-mail to a help desk will resolve whatever problems we have, it is vital to remember how important human contact is for customer satisfaction. Everyone knows it costs more to gain a new customer than it does to keep a current one. Everyone knows that for every dissatisfied customer who tells you they are not going to continue their relationship with your business, there are ten more who just stop dealing with your organization without notice.

What has been lost in the rush to cut costs and create more customer self-service is the fact that sometimes a human being is required to fix the problem. The following story illustrates this point.

I have purchased appliances from the same major chain store for over thirty years. During the last two years, I had to replace every major appliance in my home. One appliance, a front-load washing machine, had problems from the first week I bought it. Several times I went through the process of reporting the problem, scheduling a repair, waiting at home for someone to show up, waiting for parts to be sent and having a technician come to my home. I experienced the usual frustrations associated with changing my schedule to accommodate the store's four-hour window policy, repair people being two to three hours late, and a washing machine that still did not work properly.

I finally decided I wanted a new machine, and according to the level-three complaint person, I had a right to a new one because the old one was still under the initial warranty. (Getting to that person took seven phone calls, two disconnects and two hours of my time.)

Finding someone who would listen to me and had decision-making authority took another two hours of telephone button-pushing, searching the company's web site, and talking to people who said, "That's not my department." I talked to several people who understood my problem but had no decision-making power. I finally reached the right person, a store manager. By the time I got to him, I was frustrated and angry and had drafted a letter to the CEO of the company about how I was never going to buy another product from them. He said the magic words, "I will help you. I will make sure your problem is solved."

Here are the things he did that made a difference:

1. He acknowledged my problem and the frustration I felt.

2. He said he would find out what to do to solve the problem, and he called every store in the area, found my original order, and called corporate people to refresh his knowledge of return and replacement policy he updated me each time he found out a new piece of information.

3. He gave me his cell phone number and told me to call him at any time.

4. He arranged for me to come into the store and select a replacement washing machine.

4. He met me in the appliance department, introduced me to the salesperson, and explained exactly what to do so that I would be satisfied.

5. He thanked me for sticking with him and for continuing to be a loyal customer.

When I told the store manager that I was the type of customer he did not want to lose, he said something very interesting. "We don't want to lose any of our customers, not just you."

Have you turned to too much customer self-service? Have you made it impossible for customers to talk to a person? Have you empowered people to make decisions quickly? Have you created policies that demonstrate your commitment to customer satisfaction? When customers have problems, sometimes only another human being can fix them.

Sensitivity Training Needs To Be Revisited

I am old enough to remember "sensitivity" training's various reincarnations.

In the 1970s, it took the form of touchy-feely sessions based on the idea that everyone should be honest, open and loving to each other. In the 1980s and 1990s, most sensitivity sessions were designed to help people learn to work with and appreciate differences. This could include sessions designed to help people include and feel comfortable with working with women, people of color, different nationalities, different personality types, etc. Most major organizations provided some form of sensitivity or diversity training to their employees. Overall, by 2000, most organizations and the people who worked there had learned how to behave properly, how to benefit from a diverse workplace, and how to appreciate multiple viewpoints.

Given its history and knowing that sensitivity training can only go so far in changing beliefs and habits, I was only mildly surprised when two events happened in the past year. One had to do with a foreign-owned organization that operates in the United States. The other event happened in an American-owned and -operated organization. Both events made me realize that it might be time to re-package and re-offer sensitivity training.

The first incident was interesting because the organization's leader wanted to improve the way managers related to people of color. In his eyes, the problem was clearly "black and white." I convinced him that it would be best to start with the idea that everyone is different and that his managers, who had never been exposed to this type of training, needed to understand the benefits of a diverse workforce and have an appreciation for all the ways people can be different.

While delivering the training, it became obvious to me that 70 percent of the managers were blind to how their behavior was responsible for employees' feeling that they were being discriminated against. The workshops revealed that everyone except the managers felt some sense of discrimination, and this included the women managers. Although no one espoused prejudice, behaviors such as yelling, sarcasm, lack of empathy and assignment of work lead to the employees' grievances. I concluded that until the managers truly understood the relationship between their overt behaviors and how employees felt, the problem would never go away.

The second example was interesting because the organization's employees were highly diverse in race, gender, country of origin, age and other factors. In this case, I never expected to see problems with diversity. I was wrong. My first view of the problem came when one of the managers asked to speak to me about his struggles with being non-American-born. He, and many people in his department, were from a different country and for many, English was their second language. He felt that he and his department were treated with disrespect. He wanted to know what he should do to combat this disrespect and improve his department's image with the rest of the organization.

The incident occurred when I observed one of his managers' behaviors with his team. This person had difficulty speaking clear English and rather than take advantage of offers from the company to send him to training, he acted defensive and angry. He was curt with people, raised his voice, and chronically showed up late for meetings. People did treat him with disrespect, not because of his nationality, but because of his behavior.

Then an incident happened to me. After completing a training session, I gave out the usual training evaluation form for all participants to complete. One of the participants, who refused to complete assignments, had not liked the feedback I had given him during the session. On his feedback form, he described my training style in a name-calling, highly offensive way. When discussing this incident with the person's manager, the manager made an interesting comment. He said, "It seems like every few years we need to do sensitivity training for people. Some seem to forget what they learned."

The bottom line is that whatever we want to call it, teaching people to be sensitive to others and to act in a way that demonstrates respect should be ongoing. Successful organizations are diverse, and these organizations teach and reinforce behaviors that demonstrate the appreciation of diversity. Make sure your organization is one of these.

Helene F Uhlfelder PhD

Consultants Should Have Expertise Warning Labels

Twice in the last three weeks, I received phone calls from consultants I previously worked with at information technology-related consulting companies. The first call was from a CEO who was given my name by a gentleman who worked on a project with me when I ran the change management and organization design practice of a mid-size consulting company.

First call: "Helene, we are in the middle of a project to implement XYZ software in locations all over the world. We now need job descriptions and organization structures changed. We have asked the client's human resources group to help us with this, but they just stare at us bleary-eyed. We have done as much as we are able to do with our current consultants."

Second call: "Helene, I wanted to know if you are available to review some work we have done for a client on redesigning their organization. We have already taken one team of consultants off this project because they did not know what to do. We have a second team completing the work now, and I am not happy with what they produced."

In both situations, a client engaged the two consulting firms to complete specified deliverables: new marketing strategy and organization and redesigned processes and one common worldwide retail tracking and merchandising system. Although I have not seen the written agreements for either project, I can guess that the hired consulting firm made reference to assisting with change management and organization design. I am also sure that specific names and resumes were included in the proposals.

However, in neither case was the right competence available to the client without additional help.

This is not an uncommon experience. For any organization that has hired a consulting group to help with an organizational change, I promise you that people without the right competence were placed on the project team. This happens for a couple of reasons. One is that the consulting firm wants to get as much billing as possible for itself, not for subcontractors or another consulting firm. Another reason is that most people believe they know what change management and organization design are and that doing this work for a client should be a breeze. The third reason is that change management and organization design are not seen as real areas of expertise, but soft, fluffy activities.

For the client, the outcome of using consultants who do not have deep competence in these areas can be disastrous. Most implementation fails due to inadequate use of a comprehensive change management and communication plan. When people are not adequately involved in the change process, a variety of resistances and problems interfere with the implementation of new technology or redesigned processes. In the case of organization design, it is worse. If the organization and all its supporting processes, practices, training, reward and compensation are not designed and aligned to support the new organization structure, then moving people around in different boxes will be just that.

My advice is that the next time you hire a consulting group for any type of organizational change do not assume every group has equal competency in all the areas you require. Ask how many times the people on the project have actually designed and implemented the change management and organization design tasks. It is OK to tell the consulting group that you want them to bring in special expertise in a particular area to augment their staff. The best solution may be a warning box placed on all consulting groups' literature saying: "Our approach has only been utilized in the following industries and should not be followed without additional help in the following areas."

Helene F Uhlfelder PhD

Love Your Work And Love Your Team

There is something about doing work you love and about doing it with a team of people that feels positive and powerful. I had the great fortune of reuniting with two such teams from my past working life. In both cases, I was reminded of what it was like to love what I was doing and to be so wholly engaged that time was irrelevant. It also reminded me why teams are important even if they are sometimes imperfect, and how working hard, when you love what you are doing, can be fun.

In one case, it was a local, improvisational theater that has been in existence 36 years. In the other case, it was the first community mental health center in Georgia. In both cases, something extraordinary happened and 30+ years later, we still connected. You very rarely see this connection in the workplace today. I wonder why.

Case One: From 1973 to 1974, I worked with the Academy Theatre in Atlanta, directing one of its artist-in-the schools programs where we took actors into the schools, taught at-risk high school students improvisational drama and helped the high school kids develop plays that they delivered to elementary school children. The theater also produced avant-garde plays, had a state touring team and held drama classes. The year and a half that I worked with the theater, there were twenty-five actors and administrative personnel. We worked 14 hours a day, had to attend Saturday classes and, as I recall, never complained.

At a recent memorial/tribute for the executive director, Frank Wittow, a group of us discussed the uniqueness of the experience. We worked hard for very little money. We were a team of people united for a common good: community theater with a social purpose (e.g., exposing children to the arts, dealing with difficult subjects such as desegregation, etc.) We had been bright and achievement-oriented then and were now, although many of us were no longer in the field of acting. Some had become well-known.

One of the women noted, "I have carried my work ethic with me to every other job I have had since then. Although I work in the government defense industry now, I have tried to form teams with the people on my projects. They ask me where I learned to do this, and I tell them about Frank and about all of you and about the fun we had. I tell them it never felt like work, even though I know it was grueling."

Case Two: From 1974 to 1978, I was part of building the first community mental health center in Georgia at Northside Hospital in Atlanta. There were ten of us on the multi-disciplinary team: a psychiatrist, a psychologist, several psychiatric social workers, a drug and alcohol therapist, a psychiatric nurse, a few community workers, and me, the child, adolescent and education consultant. Our team goal was to provide mental health services to North Fulton County. There were no models for us, and no one had developed the concept of "self-managing teams" yet.

But, because we had to meet our goals to continue to receive our federal, state and local funding, as a team we developed all our processes and practices. We had to develop everything from scratch. Often, we fought among ourselves. But we also supported each other, and we learned each other's specialties.

On a recent trip to Switzerland, I visited with two of my original teammates: the psychiatrist and one of the social workers. We reminisced about those days and marveled at how much we had accomplished through consensus decision-making, as painful as it was. Those first years were exciting. We were part of something new, and we truly functioned as a team. The three of us, although not having worked together in more than 25 years, could probably work together on a team tomorrow. It's like riding a bicycle: Teamwork skills come back quickly with people like this.

The bottom-line? Create a real team environment where people have some power to create jobs that are engaging for them. The people will work harder, the customers will benefit and everybody wins.

Helene F Uhlfelder PhD

Even If All Is Well, It Can Get Better

We are so accustomed to hearing bad news from businesses that we forget some organizations are doing very well.

Recently I met with a Hampton Roads business' vice president of quality and planning. This organization has spent ten years implementing a variety of best practices in quality and planning yet she felt there were additional actions the organization needed to take in order to maintain its reputation as a leader in its industry. The major problem was convincing senior leaders and managers that there was a need to continue to implement processes and programs that improve the operation and their people systems when everything was fine today.

Much has been written on the concept of continuous improvement and how it needs to become a way of life. It is often easier for an organization in trouble to rally the troops to improve processes, customer satisfaction or employee retention. The challenge is always greater when managers feel they have already changed and that things are working just fine. The recognition systems in place often reinforce past behavior yet are not designed to reward continuously improving behavior.

What can you do? There are a few simple steps you can take. The first one is to create (and re-create each year) a compelling reason for continuous improvement and change. This message should contain:

1. The current state or business need for the effort.

2 A vision of success.

3. The consequences of being successful.

4. The consequences of doing nothing

5. The specific actions you want people to take.

6. What the leaders will do personally to support this project.

Here is an example: "Although Company XYZ met its goals for last year, the competition in our business has increased twofold with the entry of new players in our market. We want to continue to be number one but can only achieve this by everyone constantly looking for opportunities to improve their team's work. We want each team to select and implement a process improvement this quarter. We will provide training and coaching to help the teams. The leader team is working on improving its decision-making cycle time. For all teams who meet their process improvement goals, there will be a reward. If we don't continue to find and implement improvement opportunities, we won't be able to call ourselves the best in the industry."

The second step to take is to evaluate your current reward and recognition systems. Do they only reward past behavior? If so, revise them to include behaviors that demonstrate continuous improvement.

An example of this is slightly raising the targets for critical business measures. This should be done collaboratively with the people involved, and these targets should be stretched but achievable. For example, one client wanted to raise market share five percent. They figured out what behaviors needed to change for all the people involved (e.g., increase the number of clients you talk to each week and retrain the customer-care people on how to handle client problems), and they adjusted the reward system to reinforce the behaviors agreed upon.

Over a year's time, the group achieved its goal. The next step is to identify another critical business measure the group wants to impact and go through the same process.

It is possible to create and maintain a culture of continuous improvement. The key is to make it part of the way work is done, to include it in the strategic and tactical planning processes, and to tie reward and recognition systems to it. And to continually communicate the compelling message about why.

Transformation Requires A Change Champion

I had dinner several nights ago with a group of people, one of whom, David, is a retired senior executive of a large international manufacturing company. Someone else at the table asked me what I did for a living, and I answered that I worked with companies to improve results in revenue, quality, productivity, etc. through a variety of different methods.

As I described some of the projects I have completed, another person at the table (a retired CEO of a company) commented on how difficult it is to make people change how they work. After listening to the conversation for a few minutes, David told us a very interesting story about his experiences and what he had found to be a very successful model for organizational improvement.

Many years ago, David ran a large manufacturing plant that he thought was functioning quite well. At the time, being ISO 9000-certified was critical for his plant's continued success, so he reluctantly brought in a consulting group to help his organization become ISO-certified.

Although there are many aspects to being ISO-certified, David said what began to change him most was what they discovered as they began measuring various aspects of the operation (e.g., cycle times, down time costs, quality and customer satisfaction) and what they discovered by examining their processes. Whereas he had believed his plant to be very good, the numbers showed gaps and opportunities he would have never seen had he not gone through a rigorous process to examine and quantify what was actually occurring. He said that by the time they received their ISO certification, everyone in the plant was involved and excited about what they were able to achieve. They knew they had made progress because they could see the positive changes in the metrics they were using.

David went on to tell us about the next step he took: implementing a materials requirements planning system (MRP). He said that people, because they had experienced success with ISO, were not resistant to implementing another improvement effort. Once again he brought in a consulting group to help and through David's leadership and associates' active participation, the organization was able to quantify concrete outcomes from the effort. From this success, he led his company in applying for and winning a quality award from the country in which the plant was located.

This story is compelling for several reasons. One reason is that it illustrates how important leadership's role is in any type of fundamental organization change. As you may recall, initially David was not a strong believer and proponent for large-scale change. He was happy with the status quo. External pressure and factors were the initial driving forces for change. However, David was smart enough to see that if he had to implement ISO to keep customers, he had to lead the effort. He was also aware that he needed help from experts if he was going to be successful.

Once he got into the effort and he began seeing the gaps and opportunities, he became a believer and a strong force for leading the change. Although it is possible to implement changes in an organization from any level, a system-wide, major transformation must have a strong, vocal senior executive as the change champion. And to be able to do this effectively means that the leader must be sincere, be trusting that the change process will produce results, and be willing to make hard decisions about how to handle resisters.

The second reason the story is compelling is that it shows how when an organization sees results from everyone's efforts, they are reinforced. Progress as seen in measures becomes a positive reinforcer for people and the time and effort they have expended. If progress is not made and if change efforts are stopped early, not fully funded, or not fully resourced, the effort will fail. This leads to more resistance the next time change is necessary. The best advice I can give is that success in one change effort becomes a strong stimulus and reinforcer for organizations to become continuously improving organizations. This is the way you can create and sustain continual competitive advantage.

Helene F Uhlfelder PhD

About Whole Systems

My belief, and that of many of my collegues, is that an organization is an open system and that benefits from change initiatives are realized and optimized by whole system thinking.

A **whole system approach** can be a philosophy for change, a tool for aligning change efforts or a structured process by which the organization plans and executes specific, integrated changes to strategy, work processes, and people/human systems. Most of the stories in this book reflect some aspect of whole system change.

A word of advice as you and your organization decide what projects or initiatives to undertake to improve business performance: always consider the impact of any change on all aspects of the business.

Creating Alignment Of The Whole System

Successful change management and organization transformation require effective integration and alignment of all initiatives and all the systems and structure to support an effective culture.

The model shows the various systems, subsystems, and external influences. The business system defines how finances flow in and out of the business, how the organization creates value for its customers and shareholders, and defines targets and value drivers that form the basis for aligning the work and human systems. The work system is the process by which input is transformed to output, i.e., how value is created for customers. The human system includes the competencies that motivate and organize people. Change any one of these subsystems and it necessarily affects the others.

Effective change is the result of aligning these systems with each other and with the requirements of the environment and business strategy.

Whole System Architecture Defined

Whole System Architecture (WSA) avoids the pitfalls of single-system solutions and addresses the reality of the organization's complexity and interdependence. Whole System Architecture is the process of analyzing all internal and external factors that affect organization performance and then **consciously** designing the organization's systems and creating alignment among those systems based on defined principles and business strategy.

Whole System Architecture begins with a study of the environment that influences and creates requirements for the organization. This study includes customer requirements, market trends, technology trends, social changes and potential changes in the economy.

Whole System Architecture requires an interactive planning process. The interaction begins with clear communication from the senior managers of the organization, the steering team. The purpose, underlying principles, strategy, boundaries and objectives of the process are clearly spelled out in the design charter. The design charter is the formal statement of the leadership's direction, its vision of the future. Whole System Architecture, when it is done best, involves a series of interactions, beginning with the steering team presenting the charter to the design team; questions and suggestions by the design team back to the steering team; a second response, and so on. It also involves a series of interactions with the customers, employees and suppliers. This interactive planning process is nonlinear and may appear chaotic at times.

After it is finalized, design charter is given to an appointed design team, or teams, that redesign the business system, work system and human system. The business system includes both strategic positioning and financial performance. Too many change programs fail to begin with the end in mind: the actual business performance that will both meet shareholder requirements and create capital for future expansion. The work processes are defined and redesigned based on an analysis of the capabilities required to perform consistently within the strategy. The human system includes everything regarding people, their hiring, competencies, motivation, organization and communication. Clearly, each system must be designed in a manner that is consistent and based on the same goals and requirements.

The design team analyzes the current or "as-is" state of all three subsystems of the organization. Goals and characteristics of the future systems are created after the data are gathered and assessed. What is most critical is that any design or redesign aligns the business, work and human systems. The external environment, customers, competitors, employees and internal culture are considered when any changes are made to any one or all three systems. These future state designs are then presented back to the steering team for approval, and an implementation plan is developed.

The Whole System Architecture process provides a way to develop a "clean slate" to build, from the bottom up, the future work and organization based on the principles of a high performance organization. The process can be modified to suit any organization or business and can be applied in any environment.

Helene F Uhlfelder PhD

Team Systems: Why Teams?

To achieve high performance, an organization must receive optimum output from its people. It must create a system in which people know what is important to the company and its customers; they are engaged and involved in achieving business results; and they understand and utilize measures to manage their work. High performance is the purpose of teams.

Regardless of the organization or industry, people are the source of competitive advantage. Teams are a critical element in the execution of business strategy, contributing the following benefits:

- Teams are flexible and are able to respond to changing demands.

- Well-functioning teams built around key processes perform better than loosely banded groups or individuals focused on individual tasks.

- Teams better support the behavioral changes required of a continuously improving culture. The commitment of the team and the accountability felt by team members greatly increases the chance of maintaining behavior change.

- The complexity of the global marketplace and the increasing demand to continue learning new skills are better dealt with by teams than individual performers. No individual can be competent in everything.

- Working on teams makes people feel more connected to the organization-at-large.

- Teams provide a forum for people with diverse ways of thinking, diverse views on how work can be accomplished, and diverse experiences to share their views and opinions on how to best serve the customer and achieve business results.

Effective use of teams is a process, not a program. It is not a temporary, short-term effort to involve some employees in an improvement effort, or a series of training sessions and occasional team meetings. Best practice companies utilize teams as a competitive advantage. They create the work processes, supporting processes, organizational culture, and management practices to support teamwork.

World-class team systems are systemic, pervasive, and self-renewing. They are built on strong principles and have a results-oriented philosophy. The process incorporates ownership at all levels and 100 % involvement.

Best practice companies have team systems that include the following ingredients:

- Every employee and every manager is actively involved and empowered to continuously improve their work processes.

- All employees knows their customers, what those customers require, how to meet those requirements, and know which measures reflect what is important to the customer.

- Every employee is on a team that keeps score of its performance.
- Managers and management systems reinforce teams and individuals for improvements.

- All employees develop problem analysis and problem-solving skills to enable them to improve performance.

- Work processes, organization factors, human resource practices, technology, and knowledge are analyzed and transformed to help optimize teamwork.

- Internal coaches or consultants are selected and employed full-time to help train and coach teams through the first stages of team development.

Team Systems: Guidelines

The following guidelines are essential for teams to be successful:

- Sustained behavior change cannot be accomplished by training alone. Training must be followed by hands on coaching for every individual to reinforce and shape the desired skills for lasting behavior change.

- Teams must be structured from top to bottom. Teams at the first level will fail if they are not supported by a culture in which the team process is the normal way of working.

- High performance teams manage their performance and seek to continuously improve performance by regular use of scorecards and team problem solving.

Managing Change for Business Transformation

Why Do Change Efforts Fail?

- Lack of a clear connection to strategy

- Lack of a compelling, clearly articulated business reason for change

- Piecemeal approaches to change initiatives

- Failure to design the people systems with the processes and technology solutions

- Lack of active, visible leadership

- Lack of skills and competencies to function in the end state environment

- Beginning communication, involvement, and training too late

- Not getting commitment from stakeholders, support organizations and end users

Helene F Uhlfelder PhD

Best Practices in Managing Change

Change must be clearly linked to business strategy

- Benefits must be quantified -- better, faster, cheaper

- Enterprise and interprise implications are understood

- Key stakeholders, customers and vendors are engaged and involved early

- Behavior changes are integrated with process and technology changes

- Leadership is clear, unequivocal and consistent

- Investments are made to effect AND sustain change

- Communication is on-going, targeted and personal (sold as well as communicated)

- Managers and employees need to be involved in the change process

- A communication strategy and plan focuses and unites all communication efforts

- All change initiatives are integrated

- Education and training must be built into change projects

- Both positive reinforcement and corrective feedback are used to facilitate change

About The Author

Helene F. Uhlfelder, with almost thirty years of experience, has consistently helped clients improve performance and successfully managed large-scale change. Her focus has been on assisting Fortune 500, midsize companies, government, and nonprofits achieve business results through strategy development and deployment, organization design, performance measurement and management, leadership development and coaching, and integrated change efforts. She has led organizations to understand and apply successful implementation methodologies that combine strategy, process transformation, technology, and people systems. Her experience crosses manufacturing, service environments, information-based organizations, the military, government contractors, corporate functions, and nonprofits.

Dr. Uhlfelder has a broad experience base having worked in multiple industries and sectors. She co-wrote three books: *Advanced Team Skills, Change Management: Whole System Architecture, and The Leader's Guide to Change Management*. She has coached senior executives as well as designed and delivered workshops to all levels of employees. Over the years, her articles have appeared in multiple journals, and she has been an invited speaker at local and national conferences. Presently, she writes a management column for Inside Business.

Dr. Uhlfelder received her Ph.D. from Georgia State University with a combined focus on psychology, adult learning and problem solving, and management. She also taught basic research and statistics. Her undergraduate degree is in psychology from the University of Georgia. She has integrated knowledge about management, open systems thinking, organization transformation, and human information processing into practical ways for organizations to continually improve and remain competitive.

She has been a member of the American Psychological Association, American Management Association, STS Roundtable, and The OD Network. She is on the Todd Rosenlieb Dance Board and has done strategy work for many local civic and non-profit organizations.

www.ingramcontent.com/pod-product-compliance
Lightning Source LLC
Chambersburg PA
CBHW021435170526
45164CB00001B/255